# You Call This an Election?

# You Call This an Election?

*America's Peculiar Democracy*

STEVEN E. SCHIER

GEORGETOWN UNIVERSITY PRESS
WASHINGTON, D.C.

Georgetown University Press, Washington, D.C.
©2003 by Georgetown University Press. All rights reserved.
Printed in the United States of America

10  9  8  7  6  5  4  3  2  1                    2003

This volume is printed on acid-free offset book paper.


Library of Congress Cataloging-in-Publication Data

Schier, Steven E.
    You call this an election? : America's peculiar democracy / Steven E. Schier
        p. cm.
Includes bibliographical references and index.
    ISBN 0-87840-895-9 (alk. paper)
    1. Elections—United States 2. Voting—United States. 3. Political parties—
United States. 4. Pressure groups—United States. 5. Presidents—United States—
Election—2000.   I. Title.
JK1976 .S36  2003
324 . 6'2'0973—dc21

                                                        2002013812

For
Mary, Anna, and Teresa
*pax et bonum*

# Contents

# Preface

The 2000 election not only revealed some glaring shortcomings in American election administration, but also raised broader questions about America's system of elections. Is the electoral college really necessary? Why is voting turnout so low in the United States? This book addresses these queries, along with other long-standing issues of American elections, including the use of racial data and census totals in redistricting, the value of the initiative method of direct democracy, and the utility of campaign finance reform.

Unlike most books on American elections, this one identifies four criteria for evaluating electoral systems—the degree to which they promote (1) political, governmental, and regime stability; (2) accountability of elected officials; (3) high voter turnout; and (4) thorough deliberation of public policy. The book is also distinctive in that it compares America's electoral system to those of other established democracies and evaluates differing national electoral systems in terms of the four normative criteria. This more encompassing approach can broaden thinking about American elections and encourage more thorough and far-reaching discussion.

For in comparative perspective, America is very much a peculiar democracy.

One quirky problem of American elections—the haphazard quality of election administration—seemed to recede a bit during the 2002 elections. States administer elections in America. Their varying methods have produced controversies, most famously those surrounding the dubious conduct of elections in Florida during the 2000 presidential election and the state's 2002 gubernatorial primary. National election reform finally arrived in October of 2002. President George W. Bush signed an election overhaul bill that authorized $3.86 billion to help states buy modern voting equipment, train poll workers, improve voter education, and create statewide, computerized databases. The new law also required states to demonstrate a low error rate in counting votes, to allow "provisional ballots" for citizens whose ballots are in dispute, and to provide clear definition of a legal vote in their laws. Most of these federally mandated changes take effect in 2004 or 2006.

Meanwhile, Florida's sorry experience in 2000 prompted more vigilance in state election administration in 2002. Only scattered instances of the problems reported in 2000 arose. Despite many close races, no state experienced a widespread breakdown in election operations. Only the governor's race in Alabama spawned a protracted dispute over the election's outcome. In that example, however, lies a lesson. Close elections invite nasty, protracted contestation, often through the courts. That means that improvements in the states' operation of elections cannot come too soon. Unfortunately, future improvement in election administration would eliminate only one of the several enduring problems of American elections identified in the forthcoming pages.

Thanks go to John Tierney and John Samples, who originally interested me in this project, and to Richard Brown, my editor at Georgetown University Press, who ably guided it to completion. President Stephen Lewis and Dean Elizabeth McKinsey at Carleton College gave me the time and money necessary to complete it in a timely fashion. My colleagues in the political science department proved unfailingly helpful, as usual. Two anonymous reviewers provided constructive guidance that improved the manuscript. My wonderful family, to whom this book is dedicated—wife Mary and daughters Anna and Teresa—proved remarkably supportive throughout my toil on this project.

I have been writing and commenting on American elections for over twenty-five years now. I like to think of this book as a long-fermenting distillation of my perspective for a general audience. You, the readers, can judge the quality of my distillery. I hope the product is at least 80 proof.

Northfield, Minnesota
July 2002

# Peculiar, Indeed

T he events of election night 2000 and the ensuing thirty-six days provide a striking example of the American electoral system's peculiarities. George W. Bush and Al Gore ended the presidential campaign with an excruciatingly close finish—so close in Florida that the state's slapdash system of election administration struggled for weeks to provide a definitive result. Florida's electoral votes, which the state had long awarded in a winner-take-all fashion, go to the candidate with a popular plurality. The candidate getting those electoral votes would win the presidency, though Gore won the popular vote by a bit more than 500,000 ballots. On election night, Bush led Gore in the state by 1,784 votes of almost 6 million cast statewide. A legally mandated machine recount completed a week after the election cut that margin to a mere 300 votes. Then the squabbling really heated up.

The strange events of 2000 put a spotlight on several shortcomings of the U.S. electoral system. America's decentralized system of election administration can produce unreliable results that make the outcome of any close election suspect. This quirky system often spawns charges of discrimination—in Florida in 2000, against racial minorities and veterans. The electoral college can and has delivered the presidency to candidates losing the popular vote. And the media often aggravate a difficult situation. They twice miscalled the Florida result on election night and frequently inflamed partisan hostility during the postelection controversies. In November and December 2000, the American election system's operations threatened political and governmental stability, producing new doubts about the legitimacy of the American political regime. This is not what electoral systems are designed to accomplish.

## THE THIRTY-SIX DAYS

George W. Bush was worried. The early exit polls from around the nation indicated he was in a very tight race with Al Gore, running behind him in the important states of Pennsylvania, Michigan, California, and Florida. Spirits sank at campaign headquarters in Austin, Texas, when, at 7:50 P.M. EST, the television networks, on the basis of exit polls, declared that Al Gore had won Florida. Jeb Bush, the candidate's brother and governor of Florida, did not believe the calls. From Austin, he telephoned his Florida operatives and received assurances that the race was still too close to call there.

They were right. The network exit polls slightly overestimated the Gore vote and underestimated that of Bush. By 10 P.M., their error was apparent, and all of the networks put Florida in the "undecided" column. There it stayed for several hours. With 97 percent of the vote in, Bush had a lead of 50,000 votes. By 2:30 A.M., all of the networks called the state and the presidency for Bush because Florida's result gave him 271 electoral votes, one more than the minimum needed to win the White House. Late Gore votes then started to appear, causing the networks to withdraw their Bush call by 4:30 A.M.

In the meantime, both candidates had engaged in a uniquely weird concession dance. Gore, once the networks called Florida for Bush, telephoned Bush to concede and then headed to a rally of supporters to make the concession speech. Gore was on the verge of heading to the dais to give the speech when his campaign chair, Bill Daley, grabbed him and explained that the Florida vote was so tight it was headed to automatic recount. Gore then initiated the oddest telephone call in the history of American presidential elections. When Bush answered, Gore explained that he was withdrawing his concession. Bush was incredulous, but told him he should do "what he had to do" (Ceaser and Busch 2001, 12). Within hours, each campaign had hundreds of lawyers and campaign operatives heading to Florida to cross swords over the recount.

Each campaign had important resources in the contest over the Florida result. George W. Bush could claim the allegiance of Katherine Harris, the Florida Secretary of State, and other members of the state election canvassing commission. They had the job of formally certifying the result.

Governor Jeb Bush would then sign the list of electors and send them on to Washington. The heavily Republican state legislature, with the power to appoint electors, also stood ready to help Bush. If anyone filed an objection to the governor's slate of electors when electoral votes were counted on January 6, the votes of the governor's slate would stand unless both chambers of Congress voted to reject them. The U.S. House of Representatives remained in Republican hands, ready to support Bush in that situation. Conservatives friendly to Bush held a 5–4 majority on the U.S. Supreme Court in the event court disputes involved federal law and the Constitution. The Bush strategy accordingly involved a quick end to the counting, a strict interpretation of voter intent when recounting votes, a heavy reliance on state certification, and a resort to federal court when faced with state-level judicial reversals.

Gore had fewer resources in the squabble. Many of the large counties in Florida had canvassing boards dominated by Democrats, who were likely to nudge any recounts in his direction. The seven members of the Florida Supreme Court, known for its activist reputation, were all Democratic appointees. The U.S. Senate had a nominally Democratic majority: although its membership was split 50–50 after the November election, Vice President Gore would be available to break ties until January 20 (Nelson 2001, 216–17). Gore's campaign sought targeted recounts, interpretations of state law that increased the time for recounts, and a permissive standard for recounting votes that might yield more for Gore.

Two controversies erupted immediately after election night. Angry voters in heavily Democratic Palm Beach county argued that the confusing "butterfly" ballot format caused many to mistakenly vote for Reform party nominee Pat Buchanan, who had received a surprisingly large number of votes, instead of Al Gore. The punch-card ballot had a row of punch holes down the middle, with some candidate names listed on the right side and others on the left. The Buchanan punch hole was directly above the Gore punch hole (Van Natta and Canedy 2001, 10–12). African-American voters claimed numerous instances of discrimination in election administration (Gonzalez 2001, 36–38). Little ultimately came of either protest. Democratic election officials in Palm Beach had preapproved the "butterfly" ballot through a legal process. The infamous "butterfly" was employed in many non-Florida jurisdictions on Election Day, including the heavily Democratic city of Chicago (Ceaser and Busch 2001, 180). And despite allegations of polling place discrimination, no sufficient proof arose to allow charges to be filed.

The mandatory recount was a machine recount in Florida, but each county had chosen its own election machines. Most counties used a relatively reliable optical-scan system, in which voters filled in blanks and machines scanned ballots. Several of the largest counties, however, used a more dated punch-card system, in which voters had to punch through ballot cards to register their votes. The official recount took a week to complete. The results were surprising. Usually, recounts do not greatly change the margin between candidates. Not this time. The official recount, completed on November 14, shrank Bush's lead from 1,784 to 300 votes—out of 6 million cast. Bad voting technology or irregular voting procedures could easily produce that result.

Meanwhile, the Gore forces pushed for additional recounts beyond the official statewide recount. Under state law, a candidate had three days (the "protest" period) to request hand recounts in any of the state's sixty-seven counties before the vote was officially certified by the state election canvassing commission, headed by the Secretary of State. The county canvassing boards then would decide whether to conduct the counts. Gore specifically asked that the "undervotes," those ballots initially not registering a vote for president, be hand-counted in four heavily Democratic counties: Volusia, Palm Beach, Broward, and Miami-Dade. Volusia, because of its optical-scan technology, quickly finished its recount. The other three counties, however, employed punch-card ballots, necessitating a slow inspection of perforations of all of the questionable ballots.

The problem for Gore was one of time (see Table 1.1). The secretary of state set a deadline of November 18 for certifying the results, one day past the deadline for receiving overseas absentee ballots from military personnel. Appealing to the state Supreme Court, Gore got a reprieve. The court ordered Harris not to certify the results until it heard Gore's arguments for extending the recount deadline. On November 21, the court ruled that the four counting counties could have five more days to finish the recount, setting a November 26 deadline. This instance of court "activism," setting a new deadline superceding that established in state law, exasperated Republicans. The Bush forces had meanwhile unsuccessfully sought in federal district court to end the manual recounts, arguing the differing standards from county to county violated the voters' Fourteenth Amendment guarantee that no state may deny a citizen "equal protection of the law."

By November 26, only Volusia and Broward counties had completed their recounts. Miami-Dade had given up, citing too many ballots and too little time. Palm Beach missed the deadline by just a few hours. The

TABLE 1.1 Major Postelection Events in 2000–2001

| | |
|---|---|
| November 7 | Election Day—Florida's vote is undecided and decisive for victory in the electoral college. |
| November 8 | Bush's lead of 1,784 votes is less than 10,000 votes, triggering an automatic machine recount in Florida. |
| November 9 | The Gore legal team requests manual recounts in four Florida counties. |
| November 11 | Bush petitions U.S. District Court to block manual recounts. |
| November 14 | Florida Secretary of State Katherine Harris sets a deadline for certification of state's votes. Gore appeals her decision and requests time for manual recounts in four counties. The official count gives Bush a 300-vote lead. |
| November 17 | Deadline for receiving absentee ballots from overseas. |
| November 18 | The absentee ballot count is announced. It increases the Bush lead to 930 votes. |
| November 21 | The Florida Supreme Court rules that manual recounts should be included in the state's total and that the deadline for reporting votes is extended to November 26. |
| November 22 | Bush appeals to the U.S. Supreme Court to overturn the Florida Supreme Court ruling. |
| November 24 | The U.S. Supreme Court agrees to hear Bush challenge. Florida state legislators threaten to send their own slate of electors to the electoral college and begin preparations for a legislative session to act on the slate. |
| November 26 | The secretary of state certifies the final count, ending the "protest" phase in state law. She refuses to allow partial recounts to be entered into the total and refuses to extend the deadline by a few hours to receive recounts in progress. |
| November 27 | The Gore legal team officially contests the election results, triggering judicial review of the voting under the "contest" phase of state election law. |
| December 4 | Leon County Circuit Judge N. Sanders Sauls denies Gore his requested recount. Gore immediately appeals to the State Supreme Court. The U.S. Supreme Court vacates the November 21 Florida Supreme Court ruling. |
| December 8 | The Florida Supreme Court overturns Judge Sauls's decision (4–3) and orders a recount of undervotes in all sixty-seven Florida counties. Bush appeals the decision to the U.S. Supreme Court. |
| December 12 | The U.S. Supreme Court overturns the Florida Supreme Court decision, effectively giving the election to Bush. The federal code provides that if a state's electors are formally named by that date, Congress cannot challenge them. |
| December 13 | Gore formally concedes the election. Bush and Gore address the nation on television that evening. |
| January 6 | A count of electoral college votes in the Senate elects George W. Bush president by a margin of 271 to 266, with one Gore elector abstaining. |

*Source*: William Crotty, "Elections by Judicial Fiat: The Courts Decide," in *America's Choice 2000*, ed. William Crotty (Boulder, Colo.: Westview, 2001), 50–51.

counties clearly used different standards for determining which under-votes were actual votes. The status of "chad," the bits of paper to be punched through, received great scrutiny. Two major flaws characterized the recount process. First, the county election canvassing boards doing the recounting were partisan, all having Democratic majorities. This was most disturbingly the case in Broward county, which gave the most votes to Gore in the recount—567—with a "yield rate" of 20 to 25 percent new votes from the undervotes, compared to about 5 percent in the other counties (Political Staff 2001, 147). The Democratic board members there changed to a more permissive standard in the middle of the count to achieve that result. Second, the more punch-card ballots are moved and handled, the less they resemble their original condition, impairing the reliability of hand recounts weeks after Election Day.

In the midst of this, a battle had erupted over whether and how to count the 2,000 absentee ballots arriving from military personnel over-seas. Democratic lawyers friendly to the Gore campaign pressed for a strict standard in accepting the ballots, successfully getting those without post-marks voided in several counties. Though this contradicted the Gore campaign's oft-stated desire to "count every vote," it proved successful until national Republicans mounted an energetic public relations battle charging Democrats with discriminating against American soldiers and sailors (Perez-Pena 2001, 137–38). Several counties reexamined the ballots and awarded some additional votes to Bush. The military ballots would prove crucial in keeping Bush ahead of Gore throughout the controversy (Political Staff 2001, 132–33).

Two additional Democratic lawsuits concerned the absentee voting procedures of Seminole and Martin counties. A printing company mis-take had omitted voter identification numbers on the absentee applica-tion forms distributed by the local Republican party. County election officials let Republican party operatives add the missing voter identifica-tion numbers. At times, the party workers were left alone with the ballots while they added the numbers. The Democratic suit sought to have all such votes thrown out, potentially costing Bush thousands of votes and giving the state to Gore.

Secretary of State Harris, in a hurry to end the counting, accepted only the Broward and Volusia results and certified Bush the winner statewide by 537 votes on the evening of November 26. She refused to accept any partial results from any counties that had not yet finished counting. The controversy now moved from the "protest" phase in state law to the "contest" phase. Gore could contest the result, but the burden of proof for overturning a certified election was higher.

The action now shifted to the courts. The U.S. Supreme Court, skeptical of the Florida Supreme Court's activism in imposing new election deadlines beyond those stated in state law, heard arguments on the Bush campaign's appeal on December 1. The Republican state legislature, also wary of the Florida Supreme Court, called a special session to prepare to name electors in the event of greater legal controversy. The Gore campaign meanwhile had sued to require that recounts proceed in Palm Beach and Miami-Dade counties. Both lines of judicial combat produced major results on December 4. County Judge M. Sanders Sauls ruled against the Gore recount appeal, citing no "credible" evidence that the recounts would change the outcome of the election. That same day, the U.S. Supreme Court vacated the Florida Supreme Court's decision extending the recount deadline and allowing the hand counts, asking the Florida court to clarify its reasoning. State judges on December 8 also refused to throw out absentee ballots in Seminole and Martin counties, despite the election irregularities. The mood darkened in the Gore campaign. Their last hope was the Florida Supreme Court.

The court did not disappoint them. It was slow to provide clarification to the U.S. Supreme Court, but swift to overrule Judge Sauls. After hearing arguments on December 7, the next day the court by a 4–3 vote delivered a sweeping decision. Reaffirming the intent of the state constitution to "count every vote," the court majority ordered an immediate statewide hand count of all undervotes. County election canvassing boards had to begin immediately because federal law set December 12 as the deadline for appointing state electors. Each county could devise its own standard for determining just what constituted a vote. Further, the court ordered that the partial recounts from Miami-Dade and the late Palm Beach recounts ignored by Katherine Harris be included in the revised election totals, reducing Bush's lead to about one hundred votes.

Benjamin Ginsberg, a leading lawyer for the Bush forces, immediately described the Florida Supreme Court decision as "so bad it's good" (Political Staff 2001, 210). The haste and varying standards of the recount, he believed, would strengthen his campaign's claim that Fourteenth Amendment "equal protection" for voters was violated by the recount process. He was proven right. As the recounts began on the afternoon after the Florida Supreme Court decision, the U.S. Supreme Court by a 5–4 vote issued a stay on all recounts. After hearing oral arguments, a sharply divided Supreme Court on December 12 issued a 5–4 ruling in the matter of *Bush v. Gore*, halting the counting and in effect awarding Florida's electoral votes and the presidency to George W. Bush.

The court held that "the formulation of uniform rules to determine intent [of voters in the recounts] is practicable and, we conclude, necessary" to satisfy the constitutional guarantee of equal protection of the laws for voters and candidates. However, the Florida Supreme Court, by allowing county variation in recount standards and by accepting partial recounts from Miami-Dade county, had violated this standard. Further, federal law set a December 12 deadline for selecting electors and "that date is upon us," so the legal deadline must put a stop to the flawed recount ("Bush v. Gore" 2001, 104, 108). Strongly worded dissents came from four justices. Associate Justice John Paul Stevens was most vehement, arguing that the majority opinion "can only lend credence to the most cynical appraisal of the work of judges throughout the land." The real loser, he claimed, was "the nation's confidence in the judge as an impartial guardian of the rule of law" (Stevens 2001, 121). The majority's five conservative justices, often deferential to state courts, had ironically employed the Fourteenth Amendment, long a favorite of judicial liberals, to strike down the Florida Supreme Court's decision.

With the recount ended, Al Gore was out of options. He gave a graceful concession address the next evening and George W. Bush got about the task of preparing his administration. On January 6, the electoral college awarded Bush 271 votes, Gore 266, with one Gore elector abstaining to protest the absence of statehood status for the District of Columbia.

## IMPLICATIONS

The nation survived the bizarre thirty-six–day drama of November 7–December 13, 2000 without major political unrest. No large demonstrations crowded the streets of major American cities. No physical violence or terrorism erupted. A majority of the public throughout indicated in polls that they would accept the winner of the process as a legitimate president, and they ultimately did (Crotty 2001, 62–70). Given this, one might even be tempted to call the incident a unique exception to the rule in American elections.

But it is much more than that. The world's most powerful democracy endured unprecedented difficulties in choosing its president due to unique—even peculiar—features of its election system. Chapter 2 explains just how unusual American electoral practices are among the family of democracies. No other major democracy has an electoral college. Instead, they invariably elect national leaders through direct popular vote. In most other long-established democracies, election administration is a national responsibility and balloting procedures are uniform throughout the land, employing technologies more reliable than the patchwork regime used by Florida counties. Given the variable administration of elections, charges of discrimination against minorities or concerning absentee ballots are sure to arise.

Ultimately, an election system serves its citizens through its reliability. Without reliable procedures, as we will see, citizens cannot hold elected officials accountable for their deliberations in government. Unreliable voting methods can hinder turnout as confusing and variable procedures discourage voters from going to the polls. At its worst, an unreliable election system can undermine political and governmental stability in a nation and even undercut the legitimacy of the regime itself. Florida's unreliable voting and recount procedures forced the courts into the fray, producing large political costs.[1] Deciding presidential elections by a single-vote margin in the U.S. Supreme Court damages the public standing of both the courts and the electoral system.

Americans are fortunate that the worst outcomes failed to transpire in late 2000. Still, the postelection news was troubling enough. Florida's election system problems are not unique to that state, as chapter 4 makes clear. The Florida frenzy shines a light on several questionable practices widespread in America's elections. Their presence means it can happen again and perhaps not just in Florida. Close elections should not be resolved by a jumbled and disparate collection of procedures and judicial findings. If it happens again, will we weather the storm so well?

In this book, we will explore the proper goals for a democratic electoral system. America's unique electoral operations feature some unfeasible goals and peculiarly unreliable practices. We can do better. The following chapters suggest how.

CHAPTER I

# What an Electoral System Can Do

M ost Americans give little thought to their electoral system. To them, it has a status like the days of the week or months of the year—something that just is. However, our electoral system, though seemingly mundane like our calendar, shares with it a very important trait. As the calendar structures the actions of our lives, so does an electoral system structure how our political system operates. As political scientist David Farrell (2001) puts it: "electoral systems are the cogs that keep the wheels of democracy properly functioning" (2). It is not a minor task.

This came home to me in a pointed way when I voted at my local precinct in Northfield, Minnesota, on November 7, 2000. My experience reflected a small part of the myriad activities that go into the conduct of elections in America. The vast majority of legal authority over elections lie at the state and local level. State legislatures establish the dates, rules, and administrative procedures for conducting the election. State laws or the state constitutions identify the administrative agency—usually the secretary of state's office—that oversees the conduct of elections. The legislature also draws boundaries for legislative districts (in many states, this is done by an independent bipartisan or nonpartisan redistricting commission) and also sets laws for ballot access by candidates and parties. State legislatures, subject to guidelines set by federal laws, establish and conduct the voter registration process. State lawmakers pass laws to guard against election fraud and to regulate campaign finance in elections for state and local officials. Local and state officials conduct voter education programs to inform people of the characteristics of the ballot and where to register and vote. Once all of these laws are in place, Election Day occurs, after which ballots are tabulated and results certified by the chief state election administrator, usually the secretary of state. My state government largely structured my experience as a voter in 2000, though at times Congress and the U.S. Supreme Court intervene in major legal and constitutional issues regarding elections.

Thinking myself a dutiful citizen, I had read national, state, and local newspapers consistently during the weeks leading up to the election. I thought I was ready to vote on Election Day. Once I received my ballot, though, I discovered I was supposed to cast some twenty-six votes. I was ready to cast my vote for president, congressional offices, and the state legislature, but I was also asked to vote on local soil and water commissioners, on whether or not to retain several state judges, and on several local tax issues. Now, I had read the papers and carefully inspected election-related stories, particularly during the last week before the voting. I could recall nothing in the papers about most of the issues and contests on the ballot. I did recognize the name of one candidate for soil and water commissioner, but had no idea if he would do a good job if elected.

I resolved to vote only on those matters about which I had enough reliable information to permit me to cast my ballot according to a clear preference. Using this standard, I cast only nine of twenty-six possible votes. What happened in the remaining seventeen contests? I do not really know, because they received little coverage after the election. British-born political scientist Graham Wilson (1998) ably summarized the problems I encountered when voting: "The opportunity offered American voters to make separate decisions on who should hold dozens of offices from president to county judge offers no real power to control government wisely for it assumes a degree of knowledge that voters cannot be reasonably expected to acquire" (111).

My time at the polls in 2000 revealed to me that if the electoral system determines how the political system will function, the American electoral system does a remarkably poor job of it. For the public to direct the political system effectively, it must do so via elections that make the choices as clear and simple as possible, and produce decisive results. Our electoral system features a remarkably complex set of choices and usually produces muddled and indecisive results. An electoral system should also make voting accessible to all eligible citizens and ensure that their votes are counted accurately. Americans are required to vote too often on too many matters and our electoral system does not make voting as accessible to our citizens as it should. As the Florida controversies reveal, an accurate recording of votes is not consistently the case in America.

This chapter explains the various functions of electoral systems so that we can better evaluate elections in America. Elections perform two primary tasks in constitutional democracies. One, long hallowed in liberal democratic theory, is to provide a means of popular control over government. John Locke, preeminent philosopher of individual rights and limited government (an approach known as "philosophical liberalism"), defined the legitimate powers of government in terms of popular consent:

> The constitution of the legislative [authority] is the first and fundamental act of society, whereby provision is made for the continuation of their union under the direction of persons and bonds of laws ... by consent and appointment of the people, without which no one man, or number of men, amongst them can have authority of making laws that shall be binding on the rest ([1690] 1993, 370).

Locke's formulation is now accepted throughout much of the world—governmental legitimacy depends on popular consent. The means of popular consent have evolved since Locke's time to the contemporary American belief that all citizens age eighteen or older should have the right to vote.

Vote for what? The Constitution established a system of representative democracy, in which citizens elect officials to make decisions on their behalf. At the time of the founding, travel and communication were by today's standards quite primitive. Elected lawmakers traveled to distant state and national capitals where they lived for several months at a time as legislatures debated and adopted public policies on the public's behalf. James Madison, a leading intellectual presence among the Founders, argued that representation was not just a practical necessity, but a vital means for improving the quality of governmental decision making by allowing officeholders to "refine and enlarge the public views, by passing them through the medium of a chosen body of citizens, whose wisdom may best discern the true interest in their country, and whose patriotism and love of justice will be least likely to sacrifice it to temporary or partial considerations" (Madison [1787] 1961, 82). Madison may have been unduly optimistic in his assessment of elected officials, but he was certainly correct that legislatures can slow the pace of deliberation over policy. Moreover, at times slower deliberation can improve the content of policy, not merely delay its arrival. We all know that haste can lead to mistakes. This wisdom lies at the heart of representative government.

The second function of the electoral system is just as far-reaching but far less obvious. Elections provide a means not only for the citizens to direct and control their government, but also for the government to direct and control the mass citizenry. As Benjamin Ginsberg (1982) puts it: "the democratic election, the most important means yet devised to enable citizens to exercise a measure of formal control over their governments' actions, is at the same time one of the most important means by which contemporary governments maintain a measure of control over their citizens" (3). By producing public acquiescence to the act of governing, elections empower governments to act. Elections also produce political order out of potential chaos. Consider the remarkable diversity of the United States and how our many differences could easily lead to less-than-civil conflicts among its citizens. One such dispute—over slavery—sparked a civil war that cost America over 780,000 casualties. Americans differ in terms of ideology, region, race, gender, social class, religion, and age, to name a few politically important distinctions, and one can point to several nations where one or more of these differences produced enduring civil conflict and disorder. Bosnia, Iraq, Afghanistan, Northern Ireland, and Rwanda come readily to mind.

The public allows government to limit binding popular judgments to elections, and by doing so, makes the disputes over differences more manageable. Ginsberg points out that elections, as institutions, have four major effects. First, they make voting, hardly a natural act for most humans (it seldom occurred during most of human history), an "institutionalized and routinized" form of political involvement. Second, they create an "institutional mechanism" for the mass public to affect the government that is more reliable than informal means. Third, elections institutionalize access to political power, creating a path to office trod by ambitious politicians for centuries. Fourth, and perhaps more ominously, elections "bolster the state's power and authority" by convincing many citizens of the state's responsiveness, thus giving the public a strong reason to obey the government (Ginsberg 1982, 6–7). For these four reasons, open, democratic elections are powerfully stabilizing institutions within nations.

## AMERICA'S POTENTIAL FOR TURBULENCE

The American case gives ample support to the proposition that elections can operate as powerful stabilizing institutions, given that the human ingredients of our electoral process are contentious and potentially unstable.

Even the hard-fought 2000 presidential election failed to produce anything remotely resembling a popular uprising once the Supreme Court dictated the outcome in its *Bush v. Gore* decision. That seems a remarkable event once one considers the traits of the public, political activists, interest groups, and political parties.

The American public is in many ways ill prepared for its democratic role. Americans today do not devote much time to the study of public affairs, even in comparison with the poorly educated Americans of the nineteenth century. As Joseph Bessette (1994) notes, back then "Americans of the time, faced with fewer entertainment options, were exposed to more serious political discussions in the form of speeches, lectures and debates than is the case today" (215). Compared to then, we now have radio, television, movies, Palm Pilots, cellular telephones, Game Boys, and more forms of organized athletic activity than I care to mention. Americans may work less than their counterparts 150 years ago, but they have many more leisure and entertainment options beyond politics.

Given these distractions, it is not surprising that Americans do not understand the essential categories of politics, such as contemporary liberalism and conservatism. Liberals believe that government, through additional domestic spending and regulation, should actively combat social and economic inequalities. Conservatives instead prefer more limited domestic government and argue in support of individual freedom. Most Republican officeholders are conservative and many Democrats are liberals. Such information is essential to understanding both the substantive goals in American politics and the activities of its players. Political scientist W. Russell Neuman (1986), examining decades of survey research data, found that fewer than half of Americans can place themselves on a liberal-conservative scale and only about 10 percent can give definitions of liberalism and conservatism that demonstrate considerable depth and accuracy (78, 18). John Zaller (1992), in a more recent study of public opinion, found that most people's responses to survey questions about policy issues do not reflect careful judgments but rather unstable, "top of the head" answers that reveal little knowledge about public affairs. The public spends little time on politics and a disturbingly large proportion of citizens have no idea what our political talk is about.

The public is also not well suited to its electoral role because of its strong hatred of the inevitable "give and take" of politics. John Hibbing and Elizabeth Theiss-Morse (1995), in a series of in-depth interviews with American citizens, found that they hate the actual process of politics—the "haggling and bickering" and constant disagreement (18). Rather than showing patience for the inevitable disagreements issuing from our diverse democracy, the public cannot stand it:

> If open debate is seen as bickering and haggling; if bargaining and compromise is seen as selling out on principle; if all support staff and division of labor are needless baggage; if carefully working through problems is sloth; and if all interests somehow become evil special interests, it is easy to see why the public is upset with the workings of the political system (20).

A public that does not understand the basic categories of our politics and hates the very process of democratic debate is not well equipped to use any electoral system.

Beyond the often angry and inattentive mass public is the smaller group of political activists who can define concepts like liberal and conservative and regularly participate in politics. These are the "usual suspects" who show up at rallies, party caucuses, and elections and give substantially more of their time to the electoral process than do the vast majority of their fellow citizens. Neuman (1986) identified 5 percent of the public as possessing these activist traits (170–71). One important group of activists, those who dominate the political parties, have become more polarized in recent years (David King 1997, 172), with Democrats becoming more strongly liberal and Republicans more fervidly conservative. This polarization is an important factor in the rise of mistrust in government and politics (175). As David King puts it: "when the parties are dominated by activists who are too often willing to sacrifice votes for the sake of ideological purity ... voters may find mistrust to be a perfectly reasonable response" (178).

Political parties are not the only arenas for the activists who have influence in American politics disproportionate to their numbers. The members of the thousands of interest organizations active at the local, state, and national levels also can claim consistent and important political clout. "Interest organizations" is an umbrella term encompassing both traditional interest groups, such as the AFL-CIO and U.S. Chamber of Commerce, and more grassroots organizations that style themselves as "social movements," such as the Christian Coalition or gay rights groups (Schier 2000, chapters 4–5). Many "cause" groups, such as Greenpeace, the National Rifle Association, and Common Cause, have successfully recruited large memberships motivated by abstract and ideological agendas.

These organizations actively lobby government at all levels and play important roles in raising funds and activating voters in elections. For many well-educated, affluent Americans, interest organization activism is a highly satisfying pastime.

Morris Fiorina (1999) describes the activists who dominate our politics as "self-righteous and intolerant, their rhetoric emotional and excessive" (411). Activists, he argues, are motivated by ideological concerns, and thus have no incentive to compromise. Why? Because "to compromise these [goals] is to remove the very motive for participating in the first place" (413). When the public expresses its distaste with democratic politics, much of their ire is in reaction to the activities of America's activist population.

Attempting to find their way among the surly public and insistent activists are the candidates for office. In America, political parties are much less dominant in the electoral system than they are in other constitutional democracies (see chapter 2). As a result, candidates in the United States often recruit and market themselves as individuals, rather than presenting themselves as part of a party slate. Anthony King (1997) notes that in America, uniquely among major constitutional democracies, candidates operate "on their own" as "entrepreneurs" (38). Candidates cannot rely on any other organization to provide them with the resources they need to win election. Each political campaign in America is a small business with the candidate as its sole proprietor. And they must work hard to stay afloat.

Most of the hard work goes into fundraising. Candidates for statewide offices, Congress, and the presidency must raise huge amounts of funds to pay for the necessary television advertising. Pollsters and advertising consultants are campaign essentials. Parties and interest groups also buy television time to run their advertisements alongside those of the candidates. The result is a blizzard of consultant-created advertising, all carefully "spun" and targeted to particular persuadable "swing" voters, that can confuse the shrewdest of citizens. As Hugh Heclo (2000) notes, "The handiwork of professional consultant-crafted politics is now probably the only version of nonlocal politics that the average American ever experiences" (30). This is another reason why many Americans hate electoral politics.

The cumulative result of a surly and uniformed public, a cadre of relatively extreme activists, and a flood of electioneering by candidates, parties, and interest groups is a remarkably exclusive politics. In the 1880s, the United States led the world in voter turnout, but it now ranks near the bottom in voting turnout among constitutional democracies. American elections involve a much smaller proportion of the population of eligible voters than they did 120 years ago. Then, a voting population less than 10 percent of whom had finished high school turned out for presidential elections at rates of 80 percent and above. Now, presidential turnouts are much lower—drawing only 55.6 percent of eligible voters in 2000 (McDonald and Popkin 2000, 966).

Why the decline in turnout? Chapter 3 examines this problem in detail, but one major reason is the changing ways that candidates, interest groups, and parties communicate with voters. In the 1880s, political parties dominated elections and voters cast partisan ballots. Thus, the choice commonly was a bimodal one between one of the two major parties—Democratic or Republican. Political party volunteers and paid workers personally contacted voters in a comprehensive way. Contact was widespread for it was difficult to target one's effort efficiently, because relatively little was known about public opinion. The first reliable opinion polls did not appear until fifty years later, in the 1930s. In the 1880s, wide-ranging personal contact by party workers—called "partisan mobilization"—coupled with a simple ballot helped to produce huge turnouts.

Now, a more exclusive form of contact that I call activation has replaced the partisan mobilization of the past (Schier 2000). Modern polling technologies allow candidates, parties, and interests to identify that small part of the public likely to vote, and modern marketing allows them to reach those voters with advertisements during their favorite television shows. If half of the public usually does not vote, they can be safely ignored during elections. Contacting them is costly and the likely vote yield is low. It is a rational use of limited resources to make your election messages exclusive, not general. This is one major reason that America's polling booths are far from full.

Beyond the rise of campaign technologies that make exclusive targeting an imperative in electoral politics, the decline of parties and rise of interest groups help to explain why our electoral system fails to engage so many citizens. In the 1800s, parties dominated the electoral process in just about every way possible, contributing to remarkably high turnouts. Parties controlled most newspapers, the major media of the time. They distributed party-line ballots that were commonly cast in public. Parties controlled state and local governments, and appointed party workers to government jobs—the notorious "patronage" system. Corruption in state and local government was widespread (Schier 2000, 62–64).

So, though parties produced high turnout, they often did so in a coercive fashion that spawned a major reform movement aimed at destroying party effectiveness. This response, known as the Progressive reform movement, proved remarkably effective. As explained in chapter 3, their roster of electoral system reforms gained wide adoption. Among them were many features of elections we now take for granted—the secret ballot, personal voter registration, nonpartisan elections for local offices, and initiatives and referendums—that allow the public to vote directly on policy, circumventing at-times corrupt legislatures. These reforms reduced parties' budgets and employees, curtailing the effectiveness of partisan mobilization. Other events also contributed to the weakening of parties in election campaigns. Beginning in the 1890s, newspapers separated themselves from parties and began covering politics in a less partisan manner (McGerr 1986, 130). Reform of the presidency and national executive branch made them more autonomous from parties and created a federal bureaucracy based on merit, not patronage employment (Milkis 1993, 113–22).

Alongside party decline during the twentieth century, interest groups blossomed. The number of organized groups listed in the *Encyclopedia of Associations* grew from 5,000 to over 20,000 from 1956 to 1996 (Schier 2000, 12) and the number of lobbyists in Washington mushroomed into the tens of thousands. In recent decades, interest groups have clogged the electoral system with their own advertisements and activation strategies aimed at their members and swing voters. The result is a clutter of messages at election time and lobbying pleas when Congress is in session. Proliferating messages, endless interest group conflict, and extensive group advertising during elections contributed mightily to public exasperation with politics, helping to drive down turnout.

The facts above in composite do not make a pretty sight—a public that dislikes politics and seldom understands political abstractions, ideologically extreme activists who dominate political discussions and prosecute political conflicts with relish, an abundance of candidates for office who carefully target their personal appeals to a limited slice of the electorate, and complex electoral politics resulting from party decline and interest group proliferation that can be stupefyingly confusing to the average citizen. The obvious question is how our electoral system produces stable government out of such unpromising components. There are two reasons. First, though the public dislikes politics, they are also apathetic about most political events and controversies (Bennett 2003). Apathy becomes a form of passive support when it prevents dissatisfaction from congealing into antisystem activism. Second, the public still reveres American national institutions despite their distaste for politics—a large majority of adults agree that our country has the world's best political system (Ladd 1998, 273). Americans strongly agree on our national identity. That is, there is no major geographically based separatist movement in the country, unlike the Basques in Spain or the Kurds in Turkey and Iraq. Americans also strongly support our regime—the constitutional system established by the Founders. The nasty attitudes instead derive from public views about government (who is in office) and policy (what government does). As long as the public accepts current political boundaries and institutions, our electoral system can stabilize the inherent turbulence in American politics.

## The Voice of the People?

It is a commonplace that elections often produce a coherent verdict of the public will. Journalists frequently refer to decisive elections—such as the presidential landslides electing Lyndon Johnson in 1964 and Ronald Reagan in 1980—as clear statements of the public's preferences for particular policies. Elections may produce stable renderings of public opinion, but they do not produce coherent mandates. The "myth of the mandate" is quite popular with the press because it gives order to a frustratingly complex electoral process. "Do the results of elections or plebiscites reflect the desires or will of the people on questions of public policy? The answer from scholars in the field: sometimes no, and we can never be sure" (Haskell 2001, 123).

Political scientists agree on the necessary conditions for a mandate election (Hill and Luttbeg 1983; Flanigan and Zingale 1998; Pomper and Lederman 1980). First, voters must possess concern and reliable knowledge about a set of issues. Second, candidates and parties must take clearly distinguishable positions on these issues. Third, the electorate must accurately perceive candidates' issue positions. Fourth, voters must demonstrate prospective concern with future policy, rather than retrospectively assessing past policies. Fifth, the positions of a majority of the electorate on important issues must be evident. This combination of characteristics is a tall order. "There is no potential for an electoral mandate unless the candidates have taken clearly distinguishable prospective stances on public policy issues, the public accurately perceives these stances and, in turn, casts their ballots prospectively, based upon the issues" (Lynch 1999, 242). In reality, no American national election has produced such a mandate.

William Riker explains the impossibility of electoral mandates in his book *Liberalism Against Populism* (1982). Riker begins by defining two types of democracy, "liberal democracy," espoused by James Madison (who called it "republicanism"), in which the voters use elections to control officials by keeping them in office or throwing them out. An alternative formulation, "populist democracy," holds that elections voice the coherent will of the people on public issues, which must be held as sovereign by government (9). The choices available in elections, however, make the populist alternative impossible for two reasons.

First, choices in elections may be manipulated by the politically powerful, producing an "agenda control" that keeps people from voicing their true preferences. Second, people may engage in "strategic voting" in response in order not to reflect their true preferences but rather to defeat an outcome they most despise. An ancient example from a vote in the Roman Senate, related by Riker (1986, 79–98), illustrates the phenomenon. The Senate had to vote on whether to free, banish, or execute some slaves charged with killing their master. Pliny, the ruling officer, required a three-way (ternary) vote on the options of death, banishment, or exoneration. He was attempting a form of agenda control to help his favored option, acquittal, carry the day though it did not have majority support. All of the Senators whose first choice was death, seeing that they could not defeat the larger groups in favor of the other options, decided to side with those in favor of banishment, and banishment won the day. In fact, a large majority of Senators preferred options other than banishment as their first choice, but the pro-execution Senators sided with banishment in order to prevent their least-favored option, exoneration, from prevailing. So, was the result the simple first-choice verdict of the Senators? Far from it. It was an example of agenda control by the presiding officer and shrewd strategic voting by pro-execution senators. If those in favor of execution had voted their first choice, the slaves probably would have won acquittal in the three-way vote.

Riker argues that because agenda control and strategic voting always occur in elections, it is impossible to discern a sincere public verdict on policy from them. Take the 2000 presidential election, for example. Surveys during the campaign indicated that more Nader voters preferred Gore to Bush. Had the agenda been altered to a two-person choice between Gore and Bush, it is very likely that Gore would be president today. The difference in the outcome resulted from a restructured agenda and strategic voting. It does not signify that the public has adopted one candidate's agenda over another. That is simply reading too much into it. Sometimes election outcomes sincerely reflect the majority will on policy, but we can never know if the aggregate result is or is not actually an artifact of political manipulation through agenda control and strategic voting.

Elections tell us remarkably little about the public will. As Riker (1982) puts it:

> Outcomes of voting cannot, in general, be regarded as accurate amalgamations of voters' values.... It is possible, even probable, that strategic voting is commonplace in the real world as evidenced by the frequency of allegations of, for example, vote-trading. If so, all voting is rendered uninterpretable and meaningless. Manipulated outcomes are meaningless because they are manipulated, and unmanipulated outcomes are meaningless because they cannot be distinguished from manipulated ones (237).

This result is devastating for the populist view of democracy. Populism "depends on the existence of a popular will discovered by voting. But if voting does not discover or reveal a will, then the moral imperative evaporates because there is nothing to be commanded" (239).

What use are elections at all, then? They often contribute to stability, despite the unpromising components involved in them. There are three types of stability: regime, governmental, and political. Regime stability results when citizens view their governing institutions as primarily legitimate. An electoral system must hugely malfunction at crucial moments for regime legitimacy to crack, as it did, for example, with the election of Hitler in Germany in 1933 and the military coup against President Allende in Chile in 1973. A nation's electoral system, however, regularly influences governmental stability. As chapter 2 will make clear, some electoral systems produce more stable governments over time than do others. A nation's political stability results from many factors, including its electoral system. Less politically stable regimes feature more fragmentation, contention, and uncertainty. Electoral systems can produce results that lessen political stability without necessarily making governments or regimes less stable. The political instability surrounding the 2000 presidential election in America, for example, really did not threaten governmental or regime stability.

Stability alone, though, hardly seems an adequate purpose for elections. What becomes of democracy and popular rule? Riker (1982) argues that elections do play a vital role, but only one consistent with the view of liberal democracy or republicanism. In this view "voting permits the rejection of candidates or officials who have offended so many voters that they cannot win an election" (242). This is a much less demanding standard for an election. A coherent policy expression of the popular "will" is not required, just a decisive determination of who will take office.

The liberal democratic standard is also much more functional, given the dubious components of our electoral process. If the public does not understand politics well, they cannot render a clear verdict on policy in any event. They can, however, make the simpler choice to keep or retain certain officials. Parties, interests, and candidates will all work at agenda control during the election and will encourage strategic voting that is to their advantage. This makes any attempt to read a policy verdict into an election an impossibility, because it is an artifact of strenuous attempts at manipulation by political elites.

Therefore, elections can be very worthwhile institutions. They stabilize and regularize popular participation in government, and can provide decisive results about which leaders will direct the government. That is, following Locke, a form of popular consent that provides the governmental stability in which individual rights can flourish. But that is the extent of their utility. They cannot deliver coherent public verdicts on matters of policy. This problem makes the recent rise of direct democracy, through the widespread use of initiatives and referendums in which voters decide directly on policy, a turn for the worse for our electoral system. This argument is elaborated in chapter 5. Given the limitations of elections, what can we realistically expect of them?

## WHAT ELECTIONS CAN DO

Despite their shortcomings, elections remain indispensable links between the public and government. To perform well, they must satisfy a number of goals. First, as just mentioned, elections must contribute to the stability of government by ensuring its democratic legitimacy. The public must accept the election result as fairly representing the consent of the people. David Farrell (2001) defines this task as one of ensuring "smooth running and accepted legitimacy" in government (3). Many political analysts also argue that elections should create governmental responsiveness to the will of the people. But how to assess responsiveness? One possible definition holds that "a government is 'responsive' if it adopts policies that are signaled as preferred by citizens. These signals may include public opinion polls; various forms of direct political action, including demonstrations, letter campaigns and the like; and, during elections, votes for particular platforms" (Przeworski, Stokes, and Manin 1999, 9). However, such evidence of responsiveness is often flawed. Demonstrations and letter campaigns often represent minority activists, not majority preferences. Elite activation can lead to governmental responsiveness toward the activators, regardless of what most citizens might prefer. This phenomenon characterizes much of contemporary American politics. Further, responses to public opinion poll questions about policy issues are not considered stable judgments (Zaller 1992). Moreover, Riker (1982) has shown us that we cannot rely upon direct public votes on policy to accurately reveal the will of the people.

Assessing responsiveness is more difficult than it seems, complicated by the limits of public interest and knowledge about politics, the frequent unrepresentativeness of political activists, and the political manipulation of agenda control and strategic voting that distorts election outcomes. Responsiveness can only be measured in elections retrospectively, not prospectively, and only through the decision to retain or remove current elected officials. The public may well select leaders based on their record of responsiveness, but it is unlikely to know much about the candidates' plans or have the ability to cast votes free of political manipulation.

Instead of responsiveness, it is better to adopt the notion of accountability as a necessary goal of electoral systems. "Governments are 'accountable' if citizens can discern representative from unrepresentative governments and can sanction them appropriately, retaining in office those incumbents who perform well and ousting from office those who do not" (Przeworski, Stokes, and Manin 1999, 10). Accountability is a much more achievable goal than responsiveness, and is much more consistent with liberal (as opposed to populist) democratic theory.

William Riker (1982) describes the sanction of accountability as not really "popular rule but rather intermittent, sometimes random, even perverse, popular veto" (244). Officials do not really represent some grand popular will—which is largely indefinable through an election—but they are very much on warning that the public may turn on them as they govern. This, in turn, can produce some responsiveness, not necessarily to majority wishes, but rather toward whatever parts of the public seem likely to threaten their jobs. This may fall short of many grand democratic designs but, as Riker puts it, it does have its virtues:

> Since officials are not responsive to some imaginary popular will, this popular participation [in elections] is not the act of making policy. At best

officials are responsive to a (possibly random) threat of expulsion from office.... Participation in this sense is then the act of placing a curb on policy, a veto at the margin. Nevertheless it is participation. Furthermore, it can engender that self-direction and self-respect that democracy is supposed to provide because candidates, trying to construct winning platforms in the face of that potential veto, also try to generate majorities, at least momentary ones" (245).

Accountability is fundamentally a method of curbing tyranny. Because elected officials must regularly face the voters, there are limits to how far they can go in attacking the liberties of others. In America, the preservation of liberty involves much more than regular elections—including Madison's "auxiliary precautions" of checks and balances and separation of powers, which are discussed below—but elections are a necessary part of the set of institutional procedures for maintaining individual liberty. The accountability function, then, is vital to liberty and liberal democracy itself.

Responsiveness is not. It is largely in the eye of the beholder, because public expression takes such various forms. Majority preferences are hard to discern, raising the question of the appropriateness of certain "responsive" actions to interest groups and political activists. It is probably correct that if an elected official is not adequately responsive, she will be held accountable for this and lose office. Note in this instance that the key public act is the holding of the official accountable through an election. Thus we can dispense with responsiveness as a central or distinguishing goal of the electoral process. It is ancillary to the fundamental goal of accountability. It is also treacherous to define and is patently unrealistic, demanding more of the public in an election than, as Riker has shown, they can deliver.

The Founders also wanted a political system that would ensure that elected officials undertook due deliberation in policymaking, so that in due course public views could be, as Madison put it, "refined and enlarged." As Cass Sunstein (2001) puts it: "In this system, representatives would be accountable to the public at large. But there was also supposed to be a large degree of reflection and debate, both within the citizenry and within government itself" (38). This deliberation is the essence of American republicanism, based on the principle that elected representatives can (and should) alter and improve public opinion rather than simply reflect it. To ensure thorough deliberation, the Constitution included a

separation of legislative, executive, and judicial powers and an intricate
set of checks and balances, making the three branches functionally inter-
dependent upon each other. In Madison's famous formulation, "ambition
must be made to counteract ambition" ([1787] 1961, 322) and through the
dueling of grasping politicians, rival yet dependent upon one another,
deliberation would of necessity occur.

Proper deliberation primarily occurs in legislatures, and it is hard and
exacting work. It requires, according to Alan Rosenthal (1998), five elements. First, lawmakers need adequate time to consider the complexities
of public policy. Second, they require the skill, often born of experience,
to sort through the various ways of writing laws to address public problems. Third, they should be able to perceive linkages, seeing how action
on one particular policy may affect policy in other areas. This sort of con-
textual thinking seldom occurs among the public or political activists.
Fourth, they must be successful at bargaining and compromise, vital
processes of democracy that the public disdains and activists shun. Finally,
deliberative lawmakers must be responsible, considering the impact of
current decisions on future governments and policies (41–43).

A nation's electoral system can greatly influence the deliberative capacities of its elected officials. The more time reelection requires of elected
officials, the less time they have for deliberation, the fewer skills they will
develop, the less able they will be to bargain effectively, the less able they
will be to see important policy linkages, and the less inclined they will
be to act responsibly for the long term. The more money and votes they
need for the next election, the more likely they are to be responsive only
to the needs of particular interests.

America's electoral system simply requires too much time and effort
from its elected officials. We live in the era of the "permanent campaign"
in which elected officials "must campaign early and often. And the easiest
way to do that is to turn governing into a campaign. There is no line
of separation. Consultants, then, are brought into the inner sanctums of
government to use the prerogatives of office to further the politician's
cause" (Blumenthal 1980, 9–10).

The transformation brought about by the increasing devotion of officeholders to campaigning is a subtle but important one. Instead of deliberation over policy leading, months or years later, to an assessment of
accountability by the electorate, officeholders now are "hyperresponsive"
to activists and interests who can help them win reelection. A large part
of congressional life, for example, is taken up with the "money chase" in

which lawmakers seek the hundreds of thousands or millions of dollars needed to win reelection. They wheedle cash from scores of wealthy, politically active individuals and interest groups for their campaign war chests.

This has occurred because, like all American politicians, congressional incumbents are now more vulnerable to electoral pressure than in the past. Voters are increasingly more candidate-centered—rather than party-centered—and officeholders now are largely responsible for raising their own campaign funds. The fundraising pressure grows steadily as campaign costs continue to mushroom. Further, certain structural characteristics of elections put heavy pressure on officeholders. Most American elected officials win terms of four years or less, whereas campaigns are getting longer and more expensive. The United States is the only major democracy in the world to use primary elections to nominate candidates, meaning that incumbents must triumph in two elections in order to stay in office. As Anthony King (1997) puts it: "America's elective politicians are, almost literally, out on their own—not only in relation to politicians in most other countries, but also in absolute terms.... [Those] seeking reelection are forced to raise their own profiles, to make their own records and to fight their own reelection campaigns" (38).

When the electoral process becomes all-consuming, as it has in Congress, responsiveness has triumphed over deliberation, producing a collective irresponsibility antithetical to the process of sound policymaking. Gary Jacobson (1997) calls this "individual responsiveness without collective responsibility. The safest way to cope with contradictory policy demands is to be acutely sensitive to what constituents and other politically important groups want in taking positions, but to avoid responsibility for the costs they would impose" (208). Lawmakers respond to immediate political pressures and ignore many important and pressing policy complexities. This hardly seems a refinement or enlargement of public views, and it is the result of an electoral system that demands responsiveness over deliberation.

The decline in deliberation has occurred not just in Congress. Enhanced competitiveness in state legislative elections has altered the work-lives of lawmakers and legislators so that "an increasing amount of what they do is influenced by the forthcoming election" (Rosenthal 1998, 195). The result is a decline in collegiality and civility, important ingredients of sound deliberation. Nearly every act in state legislatures and Congress is now viewed through an electoral lens. The presidency has suffered a

similar fate, where Bill Clinton conducted a permanent campaign for public approval that helped him win reelection in 1996 and survive impeachment in 1999 (Harris 2000; Guth 2000).

Elected officials are now acutely responsive to the popular forces that
will help them win at the ballot box. If the strategic imperative in elections is finely targeted efforts to activate the swing voters, the comparable
imperative in governing is responsiveness to those activists and interests
that supply the essential resources for successful electoral targeting. Responsiveness as currently practiced is not a worthwhile goal for America's
electoral system: it is a form of responsiveness that comes at the expense
of broader democratic accountability. By responding to the correct political elites, elections can be won without public accountability. Limited
turnout from those to whom elected officials have proven responsive is a
low-risk formula for reelection. Thus, politics becomes more exclusive,
less deliberative, and less responsible. Perhaps this trend lies behind much
of the public revulsion with "politics as usual."

## WHAT AN ELECTORAL SYSTEM CAN DO

An electoral system's central objectives must be political order, high voting participation, liberty, and accountability. A bevy of uncomfortable
facts prevent us from expecting more. Citizens do not have coherent policy attitudes and do not seem interested in deliberating in public to refine
them—after all, they hate the deliberative aspects of governmental institutions (Hibbing and Theiss-Morse 1995). Mandate elections cannot exist
because of the arts of electoral manipulation. Responsiveness, in practical
terms, gives unrepresentative elites an advantage—and those elites already
have too much voice in the electoral process. Thus, we are left with the
primary electoral goal of the "protection of individuals and groups from
tyrannical exploitation by government" (Katz 1997, 309).

Many political analysts consider this far too modest a purpose, and propose additional standards by which elections should be judged. Theorists
of participatory democracy believe great benefits derive from greater direct
participation of citizens in government. Richard Katz (1997, 67–69) summarizes the four goals of participatory democrats: First, "popular participation is the best way for both leaders and for the people to discover what
the people want." This assumes that the public has the time and motivation to deliberate and discover their true agenda. Second, "widespread participation will ensure that all relevant interests are considered." That's true

only if the motivation for presenting each interest is spread more or less evenly across the population. Third, "participation may increase the legitimacy, acceptance and enforceability of policies, in part because decisions made in light of popular participation should be more in keeping with the desires of the people." The assumption here is that representation cannot reflect the popular will better than the people can themselves. Again, this assumes a widespread and relatively equal degree of participation of all citizens. Finally, electoral politics should be, in participatory democrat Peter Bachrach's (1967) words, "an essential means to the full development of individual capacities" (4). Enhanced personal development becomes an essential goal of active citizenship and the political system. Such development requires, of course, that citizens take politics seriously enough to employ it as a means of personal growth.

The most celebrated recent advocate of greater political participation is Benjamin Barber. Barber (1984) argues that American citizens are apathetic because they are powerless, not powerless because they are apathetic. Our "thin democracy" of representative institutions and elite interest groups produces this powerlessness (3–26). The remedy is "strong democracy" incorporating many forms of political participation: neighborhood assemblies, national town meetings, officeholding by lottery, national initiatives and referendums, and other reforms (273–98). The goal of all politics, including electoral politics, is the creation of more knowledgeable, active, and public-spirited citizens.

Voting, for the participationist, is not enough: "no participationist regards the opportunity to vote in national elections by itself adequate for true democracy. The involvement of the national electorate in governing is too remote and the occasion of the involvement too infrequent for the educational, personal developmental, spiritual, and psychic benefits of participation to be realized" (Katz 1997, 72). The ultimate end is governmental responsiveness to concrete demands articulated by an engaged, deliberative, and conscientious public. The approach demands much of the public and of government.

Too much, in fact. The problems of greatly varying levels of political knowledge and interest among the public and the unrepresentativeness of political activists suggest that more direct participation may produce a government responsive primarily to the "usual suspects" motivated to participate in the first place (Fiorina 1999). Sidney Verba (1996), a leading scholar of political participation, sees no hope that participatory reforms can solve these problems: "Political inequality is deeply embedded in American society. Can the ideal of political equality be achieved? More modestly, can we move closer to that ideal? It is hard to see how" (7). Further, reforms to encourage participation make inequalities greater, because they are advantageous only to political elites: "the cure contains the seed of the malady ... the participatory benefits of organizational activity are being reaped by those who are already politically involved" (Verba, Schlozman, and Brady 1997 78).

The goal of responsiveness through popular participation ultimately is a will o' the wisp. Widespread citizen apathy, unrepresentative political activists, and the impossibility of mandate elections make it unachievable. For participation to work as a means of ensuring responsiveness, an unattainable and undesirable political equality must be present. As Verba, Nie, and Kim (1978) put it, we must then have firm "ceilings" and "floors" on political activity. Their "floor" would require mandatory voting by all citizens (8), a controversial proposal unlikely to achieve wide favor in America. Even more problematical is their desire for a "ceiling," or limit of political influence for all citizens. They point to the limitation of one vote per citizen as a helpful ceiling, but true political equality would require much more than that. It would require firm limits on the money, time, and ideas individuals could contribute to politics—a denial of fundamental liberties.

People inevitably vary in their beliefs, thoughts, and behaviors, and this leads to varying levels of political activity. The protection of these diverse "faculties" of citizens is, to James Madison, "the first object of government" ([1787] 1961, 78). Madison notes that theorists of "pure democracy" based on political equality ask for the impossible, for they "have erroneously supposed that by reducing mankind to a perfect equality in their political rights, they would, at the same time, be perfectly equalized and assimilated in their possessions, their opinions and their passions" (81). Diverse interests among the public produce differing levels of political motivation and frustrate the goal of political equality. Individual liberty and perfect political equality are mutually exclusive goals.

Given the diversity of citizens' constitutionally protected faculties, direct democracy cannot achieve participationist goals. This is pointedly the case with initiatives, in which citizens directly vote to set state laws or amend state constitutions, and referendums, which allow citizens to vote on measures referred to them by state legislatures. Chapter 5 describes the growing vogue for these reforms. They do not make government more responsive to the public as a whole and they do not promote political equality or the political maturation of the citizenry. Many scholars have noted their deleterious effect on our electoral system, resulting from their requiring too much of the public. Alan Rosenthal (1998) notes that such public votes on policy fail to produce representative results. Those who participate in such votes are the self-selected with the time and educational training to master politics. Interest groups spend millions of dollars on ads to manipulate public perceptions of ballot issues (331; Broder 2000). This produces agenda control that distorts public votes (Riker 1982; Haskell 2001). Financial resources are at times central to the outcomes of such votes (Bowler, Donovan, and Tolbert 1998). Further, such participationist reforms weaken deliberation and lead to timid political leadership in state legislatures (Rosenthal 1998, 333–34).

The abundant evidence of the failures of participatory democracy require an alternative set of goals as we set out to evaluate the U.S. electoral system. An inattentive public may not be able to reliably demand responsiveness, but it is possible to structure elections to make governmental accountability a realizable goal for the American public. Simplified electoral choices heighten accountability, resulting in high participation in elections when voters face more manageable ballots. Elections cannot claim democratic legitimacy unless most eligible citizens vote and hold their government accountable. Americans had more ability to do this in the late nineteenth century through party-based elections. Citizens with limited time or motivation can understand a binary choice between two alternative governing teams. Such a format helped to produce over 80 percent turnout in the 1880s. Accountability also becomes much more feasible when one must simply choose whether or not to retain a particular party's governing team.

Instead, we have created one of the most baroque electoral systems in the world, making it difficult even for career students of politics, like me, to hold certain officials accountable. A simpler and more accessible ballot—through a number of reforms in electoral administration to be discussed in later chapters—will further promote accountability in elections. The electoral system also must demand less of elected officials so they can spend more time deliberating and less on chasing funds and voters for reelection. The explosion of insistent interest groups deploying campaign resources and demanding governmental action has eroded deliberation by elected officials. More participation has meant less time for lawmakers to deliberate on the merits of policy because they are increasingly consumed by electoral politics.

Our goal must be a simpler, more decisive and accountable electoral system. The history of progressive and participatory reforms in this century has been a tragedy of inflated expectations. By demanding too much of America's citizens and electoral system, they have helped to create a system that does not produce clear results, has made it more difficult to hold officials accountable for their actions, and has perplexed and confused millions of well-meaning voters. By understanding the failures of reform, we can do better.

The next chapter presents America's peculiar characteristics in bolder detail by comparing our electoral system with those of other major constitutional democracies. In that context, the phrase "only in America" is not a source of pride.

# CHAPTER 2

# Compared to What?

Americans know little of other nations' politics and governments. Recent surveys have revealed that many Americans are unable to identify other nations on a map, much less know something of their governmental systems. This may help to explain why many in the United States think of their governmental system as the world's best. America's electoral system has delivered governments that have presided over a period of liberty, peace, and prosperity, so what's not to like? An answer to that question requires knowledge of how the electoral systems of other constitutional democracies operate. This chapter examines America's electoral system in comparison with those of other nations and evaluates them in terms of the accountability, voter participation, deliberation, and governmental stability they produce.

America's electoral system is unique due to a combination of several unusual characteristics. First, America has the longest election campaigns in the world. It is the only major democracy that nominates party candidates through primaries, which add both months and expense to elections. No nation takes so long to select a chief executive, with American presidential campaigns—requiring primaries in dozens of states before the general election contest—often lasting up to twelve months. The length of American campaigns helps electoral politics encroach upon governing processes, as discussed in chapter 1. The federalism of American electoral administration is also relatively rare in the world, and only in America do citizens elect so many statewide executive officials (the attorney general, auditor, secretary of state, and, in some states, even the secretary of agriculture) or state judges (Lijphart 1999, 189). This contributes to another distinctive American feature, our remarkably long and complex ballots, including initiative and referenda propositions in many states.

Given an abundance of races lasting over several months and so many candidate-centered contests, it's no surprise that American elections are perhaps the most expensive in the world. The imperative of targeted activation through electronic media is costly, requiring a steady flow of contributions from interests and individuals. America is also unusual for its low turnouts, ranking near the bottom of constitutional democracies. Most European democracies (and Canada) regularly see turnouts of 70 percent of the voting age population and above, but turnout in the United States hovers around 50 percent (Katz 1997, 234). America's system of separate elections of the president and national legislature is also relatively rare among established democracies, though many young democracies in Latin America and Asia share this trait (Lijphart 1999, 119). Far more common among long-standing democracies is the parliamentary system, in which one party or a coalition of parties attain a legislative majority and forms the leadership of the executive branch. Presidentialism contributes to candidate-centered elections: "The combination of low party cohesion and high elements of personalism in presidential systems ensures that candidates make greater use of their own resources and personal campaign organizations" (Farrell 1997, 166). America is also one of only a few nations that elects its legislators in single-member districts through simple-plurality elections. This also contributes to personalism because candidates are elected individually, not as part of a party slate. Many democracies elect lawmakers through a system of proportional representation, in which seats are allocated to political parties based on their performance in the national or regional vote.

America's presidential system has major consequences for the nation's politics. Presidential systems are "inherently majoritarian" and disproportional in their selection of a chief executive (Lijphart 1999, 160–61). In other words, when voters elect an executive, the winner takes all and the loser gets nothing (ask Al Gore), unlike the proportional outcomes of proportional representation systems (discussed below). Parliamentary systems also facilitate "party government" more than do presidential systems. Richard Katz (1996) defines party government as a system that "assumes that elections are primarily contests among the parties that are competing for the right to form a national government. Important political decisions are made first within parties, and public officials are elected primarily as representatives of their parties" (109). One party or a coalition of a few parties can gain coordinated control of the legislative and executive through an election in a parliamentary system, and be held publicly accountable for their actions in government.

This form of accountability is party accountability. Parties operate accountably if they possess internal discipline, develop coherent governments that are readily distinguished from their opposition, and satisfy the preferences of their supporters (Mainwaring 1999, chapter 1). In a democracy with strong, accountable parties, individual candidates must differentiate themselves from their rivals based on party programs, not personal appeal. Voters can then vote programmatically in response to distinct party differences on policy (Cox 1987, chapter 1).

In America, in contrast, "voters are supposed to choose candidates rather than parties, and elected officials are supposed to be individually responsible to their constituents rather than being obedient to the dictates of their national parties" (Katz 1996, 109). Given America's federalism and separation of powers, however, candidate-centered elections make it difficult for citizens to discern which officials are responsible for particular governmental outcomes. When a bill stalls in Congress, for example, just which of its 535 members produced that outcome?

Electoral systems have great consequences for the democratic qualities of any constitutional government. The next section summarizes the basic characteristics of the American electoral system by identifying other nations with kindred attributes of single-member districts and plurality elections. Subsequent sections explain the operations and prevalence of alternative electoral systems. Table 2.1 summarizes the systems' differing characteristics.

## SINGLE-MEMBER PLURALITY SYSTEMS

These systems, sometimes described by their principle of election—first past the post—offer the virtue of structural simplicity. In them, elected officials individually win office in single-member districts by receiving more votes than do any rival candidates. With a few local exceptions, this process is uniformly the case in America. It is a system with origins in Great Britain and is preferred in the English-speaking world and among former British colonies. Among the nations adopting *single-member plurality* systems (hereafter SMP) are the United States, Great Britain, Canada,

TABLE 2.1 Characteristics and Consequences of Electoral Systems

| System Type | Representative Countries | Structural Attributes | Consequences |
|---|---|---|---|
| American | United States | separate election of legislature and executive; single-member plurality election of national and state legislators; electoral college selects national executive | aids stability; hinders accountability, deliberation, and turnout |
| Single-Member Plurality | Great Britain Canada | citizens vote for individual legislative candidates in single-member districts; plurality winners; legislature chooses national executive | aids stability, accountability; possibly hinders turnout |
| Single-Member Majority | France Australia (lower house) | citizens vote for individual legislative candidates in single-member districts; recounting or runoff election produces majority winners; nations vary in the methods employed to select the national executive | aids stability, accountability |
| Proportional Representation | Spain Belgium Poland Costa Rica Sweden Greece South Africa Brazil Argentina | citizens vote for individual legislative candidates or parties; votes allocated proportionately to parties in multimember districts with a minimum vote threshold for representation; legislature usually chooses national executive in these nations | aids deliberation and possibly turnout; hinders accountability and possibly stability |
| Single Transferable Vote | Ireland Malta | citizens rank order their votes among several individual legislative candidates in multimember districts that have a minimum threshold for victory; surplus votes from winners are reallocated to lower ranked candidates until all elected; nations vary in the methods employed to select the national executive | aids stability and turnout; possibly weakens accountability |
| Mixed | Germany Russia Italy | some legislators chosen via proportional representation in multimember districts, some elected through single-member districts; nations vary in the methods employed to select the national executive | aids deliberation; hinders accountability and stability |

Source: David M. Farrell, *Electoral Systems: A Comparative Introduction* (New York: Palgrave, 2001).

India, Pakistan, Thailand, and Zambia (Farrell 2001, 19). In addition to simplicity, advocates of SMP argue that it ensures governmental stability and constituency representation (Farrell 2001, 19).

If SMP produces simplicity, it also contributes mightily to accountability by making it clear to the public who is in charge and who can be blamed. How is it simple? For each office, one votes for an individual candidate, not for more complicated slates of party candidates or for multiple candidates individually or in some form of rank order. In addition, determining the winner is straightforward—the candidate with the most votes wins. In parliamentary systems like those of Canada and Great Britain, the act of voting in a national election is as simple as it possibly can be. One votes for one district candidate for the national legislature. The plurality winners in all of the districts then constitute the next legislature. In America, of course, SMP is complicated by the plethora of offices we must elect from the local to national level. Imagine the complexity of our ballot if Americans voted for multiple candidates in each race for the state House, state Senate, U.S. Senate, and U.S. House of Representatives.

Parliamentary systems with SMP are more stable than those employing other electoral systems. SMP tends to award the plurality-winning national party with a disproportionately large number of legislative seats. The 1983 general election in Great Britain, for example, produced a 100-seat majority for the Conservative Party in Parliament though they only captured 43 percent of the vote. Parliamentary systems with more proportional voting systems are much less likely to produce a majority-seat winning party, prompting arcane postelection negotiations by multiple parties resulting in coalition governments, often of uncertain stability. America, again, is an exception to all this. Parliamentary regimes do have regularly scheduled elections, but governments can rise and fall and elections result if a government loses a vote of confidence between elections. Midterm elections of this sort do not occur in America. America's unvarying election schedule, with balloting held for some national and state offices every two years, contributes to governmental and regime stability. Governments are stabilized by the election calendar, but a smooth functioning stability is hardly ensured by our separation of powers and federalism, which invite conflict by scattering power.

America does share a strong emphasis on constituency representation with other SMP systems. As in Canada and Great Britain, each citizen has at least one lawmaker who represents their district and can be approached to represent them on local issues. This contrasts with, for example, Israel, where all national lawmakers are selected at-large through proportional representation (Farrell 2001, 20). A heightened responsiveness to local issues helps to reflect the diversity of the United States. Conversely, constituency-based representation by individualistic candidates can lead to a government so concerned with immediate, local issues that it neglects to address difficult challenges before the nation—the problem of responsiveness without responsibility (Jacobson 1997, 208).

Many critics of SMP decry its negative effects on minor parties and fringe movements in politics. SMP greatly raises the bar of party representation in the legislature. A party receives no representation unless it receives more votes than all other parties in at least one district. SMP is a primary reason why America's major parties have dominated the electoral system for over a century. Through their ability to assemble pluralities, they are disproportionately rewarded with state and national legislative seats and electoral votes for the presidency. States have authority over apportioning electoral votes, and all but Maine and Nebraska do it in SMP fashion. Thus in 1992, Ross Perot, the Reform party's candidate for president, received 19 percent of the vote nationwide but no electoral votes because he received a plurality in no states. Such a result is highly disproportionate, but decisive, in that the electoral college has over the last 170 years always delivered a majority of votes to the candidate receiving pluralities in enough states—though not necessarily the one receiving a plurality of the popular vote.

How well does SMP contribute to the goals of governmental stability, accountability, or deliberation? SMP reliably produces parliamentary majorities that contribute to governmental stability. SMP also makes an important contribution to political stability in America, though it is not as essential to governmental stability as it is in the parliamentary systems in which it is employed. By promoting the dominance of our two major parties, SMP prevents fragmentation of America's political system, a looming danger in such a diverse country. A more fragmented system composed of many political parties would almost certainly be less stable than the present system. The price of this stability, however, is a distortion of election results that underrepresents minor parties. Representativeness and governmental stability confront a trade-off in this situation, and SMP strongly favors stability over representativeness. It does so in America by delivering consistent electoral college majorities, by producing a single-majority party in most chambers of state and national legislatures, and by creating decisive outcomes in races for state executive officers. After an election, it is usually clear which party is in charge of which governmental body, and that control commonly persists until the next election.

Citizens can better hold governmental bodies accountable with such knowledge, but other features of America's electoral system limit this ability. Party accountability is far more convoluted than in Canada or Great Britain due to direct election of so many offices in the United States. Federalism and the separation of powers are the cause of some of this complexity, but party accountability was the rule in elections in the late nineteenth century despite them. The legacy of Progressive reform explains much of the decline in party accountability. The demise of party-centered elections and the creation of a more complex ballot, both products of Progressivism, dilute the accountability function of SMP. America's complicated electoral system also helps to reduce voter participation. Plurality systems in theory also shrink the incentive to vote because of the "wasted votes" cast in elections won by mere pluralities. In many district elections, most voters fail to achieve their preferences if the winner receives a mere plurality. SMP, however, seems to have no such direct empirical effect, as turnouts in Great Britain, Canada, and other SMP countries remain at levels well above those of America.

Does SMP facilitate governmental deliberation in America? On balance, probably not, for two reasons. First, SMP makes candidate individualism possible, and with the decline of parties, that individualism has produced an increased concern with electoral success at the expense of governmental deliberation (Anthony King 1997). Were candidates elected as a party bloc or slate, it is unlikely each individual lawmaker would be as electorally sensitive as are American politicians. Second, SMP encourages a strong constituency orientation, and that, in combination with brief terms, encourages lawmakers to prefer a short-term responsiveness to local swing voters and important district interests at the expense of long-term deliberation about the public good. In contemporary America, SMP acts to discourage efforts to "refine and enlarge" public views touted by Madison.

SMP does promote political and governmental stability and probably moderately bolsters accountability in the United States. It damages the deliberative capacities of government, most likely because of its combination of short terms and candidate-centered elections. This mixed verdict must be a preliminary one, though, because SMP is just one of several possible electoral arrangements. It does have a "cousin" among electoral systems in the countries that employ single-member district elections but require majority winners. This relative, as we will see, has many of the traits of single-member plurality systems.

## MAJORITARIAN SYSTEMS

The chief difference between the single-member plurality (SMP) system and *single-member majority* (SMM) system is in the electoral formula for deciding a winner. In SMM systems, additional procedures, even additional elections, ensure that the winner in each district or nationwide is approved by a majority of voters. Just about every nation on the planet directly electing a president does it through a two-round election, with the "runoff" round featuring the two top finishers in the first round of balloting (Farrell 2001, 51). The U.S. presidential system, with its unique allocation of electoral college votes by state popular pluralities, is a conspicuous exception to this pattern. The use of SMM in legislative elections is rare, occurring only in France, Mali, and the Australian House of Representatives (the lower house) (Blais and Massicotte 1996, 54).

France and Australia deserve special attention because they are two long-established democracies using different ballot structures to achieve a majoritarian result within single-member districts. In France, only first electoral round legislative candidates receiving votes equal to 12.5 percent of the registered voters in the district, which usually translates to 18.5 percent of the ballots cast, can stand for election in the second round. This law limits the number of second round candidates and makes a majority winner more likely. The second round does not absolutely guarantee a majoritarian result, because at times more than two candidates qualify. But in the nation's multiparty system, low-finishing candidates often drop out, making the last round a binary contest between candidates of the left and right. The result is seldom a one-party majority in the national legislature, but the strategic cooperation between parties helps to form stable left and right party coalitions in government.

Australia's majoritarian system, known as the "alternative vote," elects single members from districts through rank-order voting. Voters must rank their preferences among all candidates running for the seat. An incomplete set of rankings constitutes an invalid vote. Voiding these votes is necessary given how votes are counted. If no candidate has a majority in the first round, the bottom-finisher is eliminated, and her second choices are then counted. If they produce a majority winner, the election ends. Otherwise, the remaining bottom-finisher is eliminated and then her second choices are counted. If some second choices of the first eliminated candidate have gone to the candidate eliminated second, the third choices of those of the first eliminated candidate are allocated in the third round, and so forth, until a majority winner appears. At times, the strong plurality winner in the first round can end up losing once the rank-order ballots of the eliminated candidates are counted (Farrell 2001, 59).

An example of the alternative vote in action comes from the 1998 elections for the Australia House of Representatives. In the Hinkler district of Queensland, six candidates ran for one seat and 72,356 votes were cast. In the first round of counting, Labor Party candidate Cheryl Dorron led Paul Neville of the National Party by 40 percent to 37 percent. Subsequent rounds eliminated the lowest finishers and reallocated the rank-order votes among those candidates still viable until a majority winner appeared. Through five counts, all of the lesser candidates were eliminated. In the final count, all of their votes were awarded to either Dorron or Neville, based on who ranked higher in the voters' ballot rankings. Ultimately, Neville won with 50.3 percent of the vote to Dorron's 49.7 percent. All of the voters who went to the polls thus ultimately registered a preference in the contest between the two finalists (Farrell 2001, 57–59).

Advocates of SMM systems claim their system delivers a more democratically legitimate result than do plurality systems. The legislator elected can claim majority support of their constituents. It remains a system quite comprehendible to most citizens, and delivers a democratic legitimacy superior to that provided by plurality systems. An American version of this system might involve runoff elections between the top two finishers in legislative races, or a rank-order ballot with systematic elimination of finishers and reallocation of their lesser choices as in Australia. Adopting the French methods of presidential selection would make the winner of the American presidential contest the clear choice of a majority of voters.

How well do majoritarian systems fulfill the goals of stability, high turnout, accountability, and deliberation? As in plurality systems, SMM produces a relatively stable rule of major parties at the expense of minor parties. Australian national elections regularly produce one-party majorities in the lower house, and the French national legislature features stable rival coalitions of left and right parties. In addition, SMM systems can claim a majoritarian legitimacy in their results that plurality systems cannot. Accountability is also relatively clear in SMM systems, because single members are beholden to particular districts and majority preferences rule in district elections. France and Australia's constitutional structures are also less complex than America's, because neither feature both federalism and the separation of powers. This also furthers accountability. The effect of SMM on governmental deliberation is less clear. SMM seems to alter the location of governmental deliberation less than its overall amount. Deliberation in both nations is more party-centered than in the United States, probably due to the greater role of parties in their electoral processes. Australian and French campaigns are less candidate-centered campaigns than in the United States. The need for party assistance is probably greater in SMM elections, given the more complex voting procedures. Voters can find the party cue more useful in such complicated voting. However, the complex procedures do not depress turnouts; French and Australian participation in elections is well above that of the United States.

It is important to note, though, that plurality and majoritarian systems are far from the norm among stable constitutional democracies. A recent typology of democracies listed eleven with plurality systems, three with majoritarian systems, but twenty-nine with systems of proportional representation (Farrell 2001, 8–9). Proportional representation is less simple than majoritarian or plurality systems, but it does offer greater representativeness.

## Proportional Representation Systems

Electoral systems based on the principle of *proportional representation* (PR) produce governmental systems in which deliberation and bargaining are paramount. R. Bingham Powell (2000) describes the vision underlying the principle of proportional representation: "the election brings representative agents of all the factions in the society into the policy-making arena. These agents then bargain in a flexible and accommodative fashion. [This] emphasizes the representation of all points of view brought into an arena of shifting policy coalitions" (6). In contrast to majoritarian or plurality systems that encourage the decisive election of governing "teams" from major parties to rule the country, PR emphasizes inclusiveness and deliberation by representing minor parties in the legislature and often in the major decisions of government itself.

PR systems come in two forms: the common "list" system in which candidates are elected from party lists in multimember districts and the single-transferable–vote system used in Ireland and Malta. This simple description of the list system masks a large variety of structural variations employed across nations. Israel and the Netherlands have national PR, in which nationwide votes for party lists of candidates allocate national legislative seats proportionally among the parties. National PR produces the most accurate proportional allocation among the seats, but deprives citizens of the local basis of representation found in constituencies. Other nations create several legislative districts that each select multiple legislators, with the election decided proportionately among the competing parties and their lists of candidates. In some PR nations, parties create a "closed list" of candidates in which winners are chosen for office off of the party lists in rank order. Most PR nations use the "open list" ballot in which voters can vote for the party slate or for individual candidates, with parties winning seats based on the total of candidate and individual votes (Farrell 2001, 82–83). Individual candidates can move up the list and into office with a large personal vote. Electing lawmakers in this way is a complex process, because PR systems employ minimum vote thresholds to win seats and complicated formulae for allocating seats among the parties, which vary greatly from nation to nation.

Advocates of PR systems emphasize the fairness of the proportional results and the responsiveness of the broader range of representation in government (Katz 1996, 74). PR encourages multipartyism by setting relatively low vote thresholds for parties (such as 5 percent) to win representation in legislatures. Parties that would have no governmental role in plurality and majoritarian systems can hold great power in PR systems. This does spawn more diverse viewpoints in government and more deliberation among a wider range of views, but at the cost of governmental stability and accountability (Katz 1996, 74). The SMP system in parliamentary nations consistently produces stable governments, but the governmental stability of nations with PR systems is more mixed (Lijphart 1999). Governmental coalitions in PR systems can be complex and brittle— defection of a single party can cause a government to dissolve. Holding elaborate coalitions accountable poses challenges for voters. In legislatures with three or more parties—often as many as eight or ten—it is frequently not clear on election night which parties will coalesce to form a parliamentary majority that will govern the executive branch. Lengthy negotiations among multiple parties result, leaving voters with a sense of suspense about the ultimate outcome of the election. How can a voter hold a government accountable when the impact of his vote upon the composition and policies of the next government is unclear?

Also lost in PR systems is the local basis of representation that single-member districts provide. Single-member districts encourage voters to evaluate accountability and deliberation in terms of individual, not party performance. It also facilitates the candidate-centered politics of activation and helps to perpetuate low turnout in America (Schier 2000). Party-based PR systems have on average higher turnout than America, but not substantially higher turnout than the single-member systems of France, Australia, and Canada. Therefore, as noted before, it's difficult to blame single-member districts for the problem of low turnout.

A PR electoral system in America probably would produce multiparty-ism and more bargaining and deliberation among the multiple parties in state and national legislatures. It would accentuate our national diversity, producing longer governmental deliberations and perhaps less clear responsibility for policy outcomes. More diverse representation in legislatures might reduce political stability in America by increasing conflict along racial, ethnic, and regional lines. Less political stability might not, however, translate into less governmental stability. Governments would continue to operate on their calendar of fixed terms, and the separation of powers would prevent the executive government from falling due to a vote of "no-confidence" in the legislature, as can happen in parliamentary systems. PR might stimulate higher voter participation in the United States because each vote is more likely to matter in electing legislators under a scheme of proportional allocation. In addition, lower thresholds for representation may require candidates and parties to broaden their electoral targeting to win office by attracting new voters. The rewards for mobilizing new voters are greater when each additional vote counts more in winning representation. Separate election of a single executive, as happens in America's presidential and gubernatorial elections, however, is directly contrary to the principles of PR. Nations with PR have collective executives made up of leaders of several parties. It would take no small change in the U.S. Constitution—and U.S. politics—to bring that about.

For Americans, PR presents an awkward tradeoff that places prospects for political stability and accountability in conflict with more deliberation and, perhaps, higher turnout. But could the public reliably relate their vote to the occasionally arcane actions of a multiparty government? That would depend upon reliable public knowledge about a set of state and national legislative and executive interactions made substantially more complex through a PR electoral system. Given present levels of public knowledge, it is hard to be sanguine at this prospect.

A CURIOUS HYBRID: THE SINGLE-TRANSFERABLE–VOTE SYSTEM

Though widely esteemed by election scholars, the *single-transferable–vote* (STV) system is employed in only two democracies—Ireland and Malta—for their national legislative elections. As previously noted, Australia uses a majoritarian form of it called the "alternative vote system" in elections for the national House of Representatives (the lower house) and in some Australian state elections. Under STV, voters choose among candidates, not party lists, and can select from more than two candidates with a serious chance of winning, unlike in SMP and SMM systems. The system is distinctive from other methods in terms of the three primary features of electoral systems—district magnitude, ballot structure, and electoral formula (Farrell 2001, 126).

STV districts elect more than one candidate (in Ireland, between three and five), but voters cast ballots for candidates, not parties. Ballots require a rank ordering of candidate preferences and voters are encouraged to mark as many preferences as possible to maximize their chances of influencing the outcome. A "Droop quota," named after its inventor, H. R. Droop, is employed to determine how many votes a candidate needs to win a seat in the multimember constituency. Under this quota, a candidate needs 51 percent to win a single-seat constituency, 34 percent in a two-seat constituency, 26 percent in a three-seat constituency, 21 percent in a four-seat constituency, and 17 percent in a five-seat constituency. Once the first-choice ballots are counted, all candidates exceeding the Droop quota are elected. When all candidates fall short of the quota, the lowest finisher is eliminated and his or her second choices are distributed among the remaining candidates. Low finishers are dropped until one candidate exceeds the quota. Once a candidate exceeds the quota, if some seats remain to be filled, the second choices of the excess votes of the winners are then counted and distributed among the candidates. This works as follows: First, the second choices of all of the winner's votes are counted and then proportionately allocated within the total of surplus votes to be distributed. This process continues until all of the legislative seats are filled.

An example of the STV in practice comes from the 1997 Irish parliamentary elections. In the Dublin South constituency, fourteen candidates from eleven different parties contested for seats in parliament. Only one gained election on the first count of the ballots. The winner's surplus votes were too small in number to put other candidates over the election threshold, so election officials instead eliminated four candidates with very small vote totals and counted their second preferences. Even after this "second count" redistribution, no other candidates won election. For the "third count," the original winner's 239 surplus votes were reallocated among the remaining viable candidates. How? All of the original winner's 9,904 second choices were recounted and the 239 surplus votes were awarded to other candidates based on their percentage of the first winner's 9,904 total votes.

This still failed to elect a candidate, so the next-lowest finisher was eliminated and her second choices allocated proportionately among the remaining viable candidates. Two more counts, each time involving dropping the low finisher and reallocating his or her second choices, finally produced a second winner. The remaining three winners were chosen by eliminating bottom finishers and proportionately reallocating second choices from among the surplus votes of the previous winners. In all, the process took seven rounds of counting (Farrell 2001, 133–36). In multiple-member districts, this is not a simple process!

The STV system weakens party control over elections by allowing voters to choose among individual candidates. It encourages candidates from the same party to campaign against each other, hindering party cohesion (Katz 1996, 78). STV must be limited to small districts electing relatively few candidates or else the task of rank ordering candidates can become overwhelming. New York State experimented with STV for municipal elections in the 1930s, and in one Brooklyn election, ninety-nine candidates put forward their names, producing a ballot four feet long (Hermens 1984). If the system is designed to provide smaller districts, each of which elects relatively few lawmakers, the individual lawmaker's link to the constituency can be a strong one. The smaller the district using STV, though, the less proportional the overall national result. The system in sum provides "only a modest degree of proportionality and relatively uncohesive parties" (Katz 1996, 78).

STV's individualistic elections can weaken the accountability of the electoral system by encouraging the sort of candidate-centered campaigns that now exist in America. This is not inevitably the case, however. Malta features a strong two-party system and high levels of party voting with a STV system (Hirczy 1995). It also has the world's highest electoral turnout, in part because every vote can be important in determining legislative representation through STV's rank-order counting. STV also seems to contribute to governmental stability; both Ireland and Malta persist as secure systems with two dominant parties. It's difficult to determine a strong effect on governmental deliberation from the STV. The system encourages both proportionality and electoral individualism, probably yielding mixed results in governmental deliberation. The STV seems to suit many desirable electoral goals well, and it is a wonder that it hasn't been adopted more widely.

## THE MIXED SYSTEMS

Electoral systems are *mixed* if they elect legislators through both single-member districts and party lists (Farrell 2001, 98). The long-standing example of a successful and stable mixed system is the Federal Republic of Germany, which was able to undergo a wrenching merger with East Germany while retaining a smoothly functioning electoral system. Since 1953, German elections have operated through a *mixed-member–proportional* (MMP) system in which half of national and state legislators win office through plurality election in single-member districts and half are selected through state-level proportional representation. The PR is a closed list system, with candidates slated in rank order for election in each state (*land* in German). On election night, the district candidate results are tabulated, and then the national results are adjusted through PR for the remaining seats. The overall configuration of the national lower house (*Bundestag*) is proportional to the election result, with all parties that gain 5 percent nationally receiving a proportionate share of the seats.

A recent survey of democracies found that sixteen of fifty-nine use some form of mixed system (Farrell 2001, 112). Italy and Japan adopted the system in response to charges of corruption in their previous electoral systems; New Zealand adopted a mixed system after concluding that their previous SMP system was unfair. Taiwan uses a single-ballot form of MMP, with the vote for a party candidate also used to allocate party-list seats proportionately. Russia employs another distinct type of mixed system, the *mixed-member–majoritarian* system (MMM). In this system, the PR and SMP components of the mixed system operate independently, that is, the PR allocations are not arranged to make the overall election result proportional. The results can dramatically depart from proportionality. In the 1995 Duma (the Russian parliament) elections, the Communist party received 12.6 percent more seats than a proportional result would have produced (Farrell 2001, 117).

Proponents of mixed systems hold that they provide both the constituency representation of the SMP system and the proportionality of PR, avoiding the shortcomings of either of those methods. As David Farrell notes (2001), this assumes that the lawmakers selected from constituency seats operate like those chosen in SMP systems, and that such constituency representation forms an important independent dimension of national politics (109). Neither is clearly the case. MMP systems, however, are really about proportional allocation, and no mixed system has by-elections for open seats due to death and resignation. Instead, the parties appoint replacements. In practice, government operates like the party politics of PR systems.

The effect of mixed systems on deliberation, turnout, accountability, and deliberation, then, is similar to that of PR systems. Mixed systems often feature party coalition governments whose composition could not have been foretold before an election and whose operations are at times secretive. This bodes ill for accountability. Because mixed systems often produce multiple parties and no majority party, governmental stability can suffer. The broader representation within the national legislature and in government, however, can produce a richer variety of governmental deliberations. Turnout in mixed systems is high, but the electoral structure seems to have little independent effect, because turnout in Italy, Japan, and New Zealand remained stable after the adoption of the system. Mixed systems do add more complexity to elections, but they seem to offer few effects distinct from PR upon government and elections.

America has its own "mixed" system, but far different from those just described. Its combination of federalism, separation of powers, regularly scheduled elections, electoral college selection of the president, and single-member districts produces a stew quite unlike the various sorts of electoral systems discussed here. Before summarizing America's position in this broader analysis, it is necessary to reveal yet another American oddity: our system of campaign finance.

## Campaign Finance across Nations

Election spending is a famously complex topic, and campaign finance laws vary greatly across the world's group of constitutional democracies. Still, we can identify three dimensions of regulating "political money" in these nations. First, some nations provide subsidies of varying size to parties and/or candidates, and some do not. Second, nations vary in whether they impose limits on campaign expenditures and contributions, and on the amount of those limits. Third, regulations requiring the disclosure of campaign spending and contributions vary across nations.

America has highly distinctive campaign finance rules and practices. Federalism creates fifty different sets of campaign finance rules for elections of state and local government officials. All states have some sort of disclosure requirements for campaign spending and contributions. Some states leave their elections privately financed without spending limits, and some—such as Minnesota, Vermont, and Maine—provide public subsidies to candidates in return for the candidate abiding by spending limits. In these partially public-financed systems, candidates must have the option of forgoing public financing and raising funds privately in unlimited amounts, due to the 1976 U.S. Supreme Court's decision in *Buckley v. Valeo*, which created the foundation of American state and national campaign finance. To understand American campaign finance, we must start with this decision.

In *Buckley* the Court established three constitutional principles for campaign finance. First, the court struck down campaign expenditure limits passed by Congress in the early 1970s. The decision left three sorts of expenditures unlimited: (1) the amount of her own money a candidate spends on her own behalf, (2) the amount a candidate legally raises and spends on her own behalf, and (3) the total "independently expended" by interest groups in election campaigns as long as it is not coordinated with candidates. The Court held that such limits restricted free expression guaranteed by the First Amendment: "the concept that the government may restrict the speech of some elements of our society in order to enhance the relative voice of others is wholly foreign to the First Amendment" (*Buckley* 48–49).

Second, the Court upheld disclosure laws that require full accounting of funds received and expended by candidates, and also validated contribution limits. By law, individuals then could only contribute $1,000 per candidate per election (meaning $1,000 for the primary and $1,000 for the general election) and political action committees (regulated by law and usually formed by interest groups as a legal funnel for funds to candidates) could give a maximum of $5,000 per candidate per election. The Court held that limiting contributions and requiring disclosure were necessary to avoid actual corruption or the "appearance of corruption" in campaigns (*Buckley* 28). A campaign finance law in 2002 raised the individual limits to $2,000 per candidate per election and indexed future contributions to the inflation rate. The law also restricts certain forms of interest group spending on campaign advertisements (see chapter 6).

Third, the Court upheld a system for public finance of presidential election campaigns passed into law in the early 1970s. Under this law, candidates for the presidential nominations in their party's primaries who qualified could receive matching public funds equal to the first $250 contributed by each individual. In return, the candidates had to abide by federally imposed spending requirements in each of the primary states. In the general election campaign, the major party nominees are offered near-total public financing if they will accept campaign-spending limits. This principle limits the permissible extent of public financing in American elections today. The Court allows states (and, in theory, the federal government, though Congress has passed no such law) to offer public financing to candidates, but candidates must retain the choice of raising and spending unlimited funds privately. In this, America differs from several nations that strictly limit campaign expenditures (LeDuc, Niemi, and Norris 1996, 38–44).

Recent campaign practices, discussed further in chapter 6, have effectively voided the limits on political party spending Congress put in place in the 1970s, helping to raise the cost of American national elections enormously in recent years. Now, America's electoral system is "among the most expensive in the world" (Anthony King 1997, 41). Huge amounts of funds go into a blizzard of campaign advertisements sponsored by a bevy of interest groups, candidates, and parties. It is a confusing information tsunami unlike any other election season in the world, producing cries for campaign finance reform. It is unclear if the 2002 reforms, which will go into effect for the 2004 elections, will improve the situation.

The cash explosion in American elections is distinctive because the United States is alone among seventeen major democracies in providing neither limits on campaign spending nor subsidies for the use of television time by candidates and parties (LeDuc, Niemi, and Norris 1996, 38–47). Candidates, parties, and interests can spend unlimited funds on television, none of which is provided free. And do they!

Only four of forty-five major constitutional democracies provide no free television airtime (the United States, Mexico, Norway, and Taiwan). Only eight of twenty-seven democracies provide no direct public subsidies to either political parties or individual candidates. Merely five of the seventeen democracies for which we have data have no limit on campaign spending (LeDuc, Niemi, and Norris 1996, 45–48). America's combination of minority characteristics makes its elections unique in the world.

America's privately funded and lightly regulated national legislative elections probably resemble the fabled "Wild West" to many foreign observers. The striking result of all this free spending, however, is remarkably low turnout. Candidates, parties, and interests are free to use great amounts of funds to target and activate small parts of the public who are decisive in election campaigns (Schier 2000). More spending does not mean greater citizen engagement. America's electoral failures are most conspicuous regarding this important democratic goal.

American campaign finance contributes mightily to the many shortcomings of the nation's electoral system in turnout, accountability, stability, and deliberation. Carefully targeted spending hardly boosts turnout. The cacophony of well-funded voices—from candidates, parties, and interests—during election time makes it difficult for voters to determine whom to hold accountable for the actions of government. This is perhaps more a problem of America's baroque ballot, because fewer candidates running for fewer offices would make accountability decisions easier for all citizens. Still, all the noise complicates the task. The constant need for campaign money, noted in chapter 1, requires lawmakers to spend more time on fundraising and less on deliberation over public policy. How does American campaign finance affect stability? Not governmentally, but politically. It doesn't alter the security of fixed terms, but it does require most state and national lawmakers to "run scared" because of the chronic electoral risks engendered by such an expensive, crowded campaign environment (Anthony King 1997).

Other nations contain the negative effects of campaign finance on governing by adopting one or more of four approaches: (1) limiting how much can be raised, (2) limiting how much can be spent, (3) cutting the cost of campaigns through public subsidies to parties (Japan is the only nation that gives subsidies directly to national legislative candidates), and (4) reducing the cost of advertising through free television airtime. The United States employs none of these approaches. Thus, in America governing is more about getting elected, and getting elected is more about raising money than it is in other democracies. America's distinctive method of campaign finance does its electoral system and the quality of American democracy itself no favors.

## In Composite

Which sort of electoral system best meets the goals of governmental stability, high turnout, accountability, and deliberation? The answer is far from obvious. The empirical record gives clear signals about the effects of system structure on governmental stability and turnout. SMP and SMM systems seem to promote stability and accountability, but they have no clear advantage over other systems in deliberation and turnout. It is hard to assess the impact of the various electoral systems on accountability and deliberation. David Farrell (2001), however, provides some useful distinctions for that task. Farrell argues that nations with candidate-centered elections produce more of an emphasis on a "delegate" style by lawmakers (171). A delegate views her job as one of faithfully representing the views of what she takes to be her important constituents. Party-based elections, in contrast, produce legislators with more of a "trustee" style. A "trustee" is primarily concerned with using her best judgment on matters of policy rather than representing constituents.

As Edmund Burke ([1774] 1999), the great English parliamentarian who first espoused this style, put it: "Parliament is a deliberative assembly of one nation, with one interest, that of the whole—where not local purposes, not local prejudices, ought to guide, but the general good, resulting from the general reason of the whole" (374). The "refining and enlarging" of public sentiments through deliberation lies at the root of the trustee style. By this measure, the American electoral system performs poorly at deliberation, delivering a "responsiveness without responsibility" on policy far too often. Farrell (1997) notes that European democracies—whether SMP, SMM, PR, mixed, or STV—tend to feature party-based campaigns, whereas America's electoral system is as candidate-based as any in the world (164–65). Japan is the only other major democracy with an electoral system as candidate-based as America's. That trait, combined with a SMP system of electing legislators, produces American governments that seek less to deliberate than to accommodate the immediate demands of voters and interests before the next election. Accountability becomes an individual matter for elected officials, and less of a collective party concern. Though this facilitates the accountability of individual legislators, it attenuates greatly the ability of voters to hold the government collectively accountable. In sum, though the American electoral system does provide governmental stability through its regularly scheduled elections and SMP operations, it falls far short of the ideal in accountability, deliberation, and turnout.

None of the rival electoral systems, however, are dramatically superior on all of the four goals mentioned above. SMP parliamentary systems do provide greater governmental stability than other parliamentary variants. They also make accountability simple through the casting of a single vote for a single candidate for the national legislature. Because the systems are party-based, more collective deliberation occurs than in America. The simplicity of voting in an SMP system might make turnout higher, but SMP systems don't rank distinctively above other systems in turnout. The SMM systems of France and Australia produce the same effects on governmental stability, turnout, accountability, and deliberation, but can claim superior democratic legitimacy through their system of majority election.

PR parliamentary systems offer less governmental stability because they facilitate the expression of greater societal and governmental pluralism. In theory, each vote under PR counts more in determining the composition of the legislature than in SMP and SMM systems, but one finds high turnouts in SMM, SMP, and PR nations. Accountability is particularly problematical with PR, because voters do not really know the consequences of their ballots for present and future coalition governments. Deliberation, though, is more inclusive of societal diversity and more likely to be thorough because PR systems are strongly party-based. Most mixed systems also employ PR and thus affect turnout, governmental stability, deliberation, and accountability similarly to PR systems.

The oddest hybrid is the rare STV system. The STV system does not hurt governmental stability in Ireland and Malta, and it can well stimulate turnout because every vote counts in determining the composition of parliament. As previously mentioned, Malta has the highest turnout in the world. Elections are party-based in both nations, aiding accountability, though the STV ballot requires votes to select individual candidates. The STV nations deliberate in a party-based fashion, avoiding the hyper-responsiveness of candidate-centered American elections. STV, in sum, improves on the American system without possessing the shortcomings of rival systems.

An ideal American system might include the STV in single-member legislative districts in which voters cast ballots for individual candidates. The STV system favors large parties, and might maintain America's vaunted political stability. Most importantly, STV makes every vote count because even voters whose first-choice candidate loses still have their second, and perhaps third, choices counted. When every vote counts, parties, candidates, and interests suddenly have incentives to maximize electoral participation, a possible antidote to the exclusive politics of activation (Schier 2000). Adopting STV with single-member districts would transform American legislative elections into a single-member–majority (SMM) system similar to that used in Australia.

However, the choice of this STV-SMM system would be a far-reaching one, with untold consequences for American elections. How, for example, would it alter presidential elections? The elimination of Nader and a counting of the second choices of his voters probably would have delivered enough electoral votes to Al Gore to win the presidency. That would produce an election result more in keeping with the preferences of a plurality of voters. Would the adoption of the STV-SMM system be worth the dramatic change it might require in America's elections? Before passing judgment on this system, we must examine other aspects of the American electoral process in more depth. We next turn to a unique and disturbing trend in the history of the world's constitutional democracies—the disturbing decline in voting turnout in American elections over the past 120 years.

# CHAPTER 3

# Why Turnout Fell

I t is a remarkable story, one unusual in the history of world democracy. It is also a puzzle. Political science studies have consistently found more educated citizens more likely to turn out and vote. In the 1880s, no nation could rival America in voting turnout, though less than 10 percent of the American voting age population had even a high school education. Turnout in presidential contests steadily hovered around 80 percent in the last quarter of the nineteenth century (Kornbluth 2000, 12). But in 2000, a bit over half of eligible voters—55.6 percent—turned out in the closest election in American presidential history when the percentage of Americans with college degrees had reached 25 percent for the first time in American history (McDonald and Popkin 2001, 966).

No stable democratic nation has ever suffered so large a long-term decline in voting participation. The huge drop-off challenges the very legitimacy and accountability of governments produced by elections in which so many citizens stay home. This chapter examines those consequences, after first attempting to solve the case of the vanishing voter. Many forces lie behind such a mammoth trend. Changes in election rules, governmental structure, and the power and effectiveness of both political parties and interest groups all contributed to an abandonment of the polling booth the likes of which no nation other than America has encountered.

Figure 3.1 details the turnout trend in presidential and congressional elections from 1840 to 2000. From a participatory apex from 1876 to 1892, the proportion of citizens voting declined from 1896 to 1932. Turnout then rose during the economic crises of the 1930s, followed by another gradual decline to the present levels, the lowest since the 1920s. The voting drop-off occurred in both presidential and congressional elections, and the disparity in turnout between these different elections grew over time. In the 1880s, a large majority of eligible voters cast ballots every two years, whether or not the presidency was at stake. By the late twentieth century, turnout for congressional elections had declined by 40 percent from the levels of the 1880s, to about two-fifths of the voting-age population.

The turnout disparity between presidential and congressional elections is also troubling, as Arend Lijphart (1997) notes: "congressional elections should rank close to presidential ones in democracies in which the executive and legislature are coequal branches of the government.... When considering the problem of low voter turnout, [such] second-order elections with their often striking lower voter participation, cannot be ignored" (6). Turnout in the many local elections in America—such as those for city councils, county boards, school bond issues, and municipal referenda—is more disturbing still, usually pulling to the polls no more than 10 to 20 percent of eligible voters (DeSipio 2000, 312).

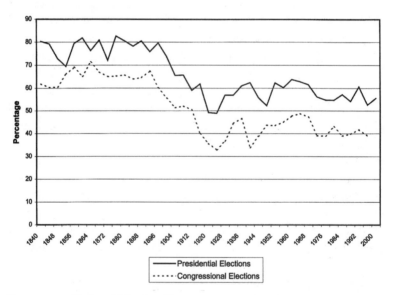

FIGURE 3.1 National Election Turnouts in America 1840–2000.

*Sources*: Years 1840–1946, Walter Dean Burnham, "Voter Turnout Rates, United States, South and Nonsouth, 1798–1998," in *Vital Statistics on American Politics 1999–2000*, edited by Harold W. Stanley and Richard G. Niemi (Washington, D.C.: Congressional Quarterly Press), 2002; years 1948–2000, Michael P. McDonald and Samuel L. Popkin, "The Myth of the 'Vanishing Voter,'" *American Political Science Review* 95 (December 2001): 966.

The broader historical trend suggests that events during two periods—from 1896 to about 1920 and from 1968 to the present—deflated voting. The first era of decline witnessed the rise of the Progressive reform movement and the growing uncompetitiveness of elections in many states and regions in national politics. The more recent period included the rise of television as a campaign tool, an explosion of interest groups, and the dominance of candidate-centered campaigns. These forces helped produce America's distinctively low turnout in recent elections.

How distinctive? Table 3.1 reveals that no other major democracy rivals America in low turnout. Only tiny Switzerland has turnout at levels resembling that of the United States. Swiss turnout may be explained by the fact that it is a highly federal nation, and national elections are not as important as canton elections in terms of overall governance (Lijphart 1999, 45, 193). America, though also federal, has national elections that are crucial to national and world governance. Because America's turnout is exceptionally low and its pattern of decline is unique among developed

TABLE 3.1 National Election Turnouts in Selected Democracies[a]

| Country | Turnout (%) | Year |
|---|---|---|
| Australia | 95.2 | 1998 |
| Germany | 82.2 | 1998 |
| Sweden | 81.4 | 1998 |
| Austria | 80.4 | 1999 |
| Greece | 76.3 | 1996 |
| Spain | 70.6 | 2000 |
| Japan | 62.5 | 2000 |
| Great Britain | 59.4 | 2001 |
| United States | 55.6 | 2000 |
| Switzerland | 43.4 | 1999 |

[a] All countries in the table except the United States have turnout reported as the percentage of registered voters casting ballots. United States turnout is percentage of voting eligible population casting ballots. The totals are comparable because registration is universal and government-sponsored in all nations in the table except the United States, meaning that the number of registered voters is very close to the total voting-eligible population in those nations.

*Sources*: International Voter Turnout, Federal Election Commission, www.fec.gov/voteregis/InternatTO.htm; American turnout, Michael P. McDonald and Samuel P. Popkin, "The Myth of the 'Vanishing Voter,'" *American Political Science Review* 95 (December 2001): 966.

democracies, we must look within the nation for explanations. But to understand how to maintain high turnout, we will later examine the election rules—particularly regarding voter registration and election proportionality—that have helped other nations maintain high turnouts. One way to begin sorting out America's voting slump is to identify the reasons why turnout was so high in the nineteenth century.

## When Everybody Voted

Voter turnout was virtually universal in the America of the 1870s and 1880s. Given that personal illness, changes of residence, and the difficulty of voting in rural areas would inevitably keep turnout below 100 percent, "late-nineteenth-century voter turnouts were virtually complete" (Kornbluth 2000, 21). Beyond voting, political participation also persisted at very high levels. Historian Michael McGerr estimates that more than one-fifth of voters in northern states played an active role in party-sponsored campaign organizations (McGerr 1986, 26). No other nation on the planet had such widespread electoral participation.

America's strong political parties of the time explain much of the high electoral participation. Back then, "political parties dominated. They shaped everything that went on, and gave life, depth and intensity to the system" (Silbey 1991, 211). Legislatures were the dominant branches of state and national governments. Within legislatures, party voting was common and party leaders dominated operations. In elections, the public voted straight party tickets with few exceptions. As Josiah Strong noted in 1890, "The vast majority of voters on both sides are party men who vote the same way year after year" (quoted in Kleppner 1982, 113). Party organizations dominated electoral operations. "Among other things, they registered voters, printed, distributed and counted ballots; nominated candidates; financed and ran campaigns; and controlled the distribution of political information through an overwhelmingly partisan press" (Kornbluth 2000, 41). Explaining the high turnout requires understanding how parties reached such a pinnacle of power in the 1870s and 1880s.

Alan Ware (1988) provides a sound definition of party strength. A strong party "can determine who will be the party's candidates, can decide (broadly) the issues on which electoral campaigns will be fought by its candidates, contributes the 'lion's share' of resources to candidates' election campaigns and has influence over the appointments made by elected public officials" (x). American parties commanded all of these powers in the late nineteenth century. They have very little of such authority left today. The decline of parties parallels the decline in turnout and is a major reason why more and more citizens abandoned the polling booth.

Parties were strong in the late nineteenth century because they proved to be useful instruments for politicians to employ in achieving their goals. Electoral politicians have three primary goals: gaining reelection, making substantively good public policy, and achieving influence within government (Fenno 1973). John Aldrich (1995) argues that "ambitious politicians turn to the political party to achieve such goals only when parties are useful vehicles for solving problems that cannot be solved effectively, if at all, by other means" (5). Unlike today, parties in the late 1800s proved very useful to politicians in attaining their goals. Politicians could effectively pursue their goals through "one stop shopping" with the party of their choice. Party organizations provided nominations for office, had loyal voters ready to vote for the nominee, funded the campaigns, and even administered the process of voting at the polls on Election Day. In government, they determined the distribution of authority within legislatures and had great influence over many executive branch appointments. Parties controlled thousands of patronage jobs in state, local, and national government, given the loyal party workers as a material award for service. Nearly all of the ambitious politicians of the 1870s and 1880s worked through the major parties to achieve their goals.

Voters found parties quite useful as well. The electorate, comprised of many new immigrants to America, was not well educated. The electorate grew enormously during this period, expanding 50 percent from 1880 to 1896 (Kornbluth 2000, 40). Fewer than one in ten voters even had a high school education. Many voters needed guidance in navigating America's complex elections, and political parties provided that guidance. By casting a simple party-line vote, a new voter could pick a governing team with which he agreed on policy and that often provided voters with material benefits in the form of government jobs, local services, and even an Election Day financial bonus.[1] Parties also provided a major form of inclusive popular entertainment in the form of partisan rallies, parades, picnics, and banquets. In an era before television, radio, or movies, such local celebrations allowed voters to socialize and relax at party expense. Party events drew large and diverse crowds. Moisei Ostrogorski (1902), a political scientist of the time, described an inclusive partisan celebration: "all classes of the population are represented, from the princes of finance down to the common people; heads of business firms and members of the bar fall in, shouting themselves hoarse, in honor of the candidates of the party, just like ordinary laborers" (2:333–34).

The two major political parties were strongly competitive in each region of the country in the 1870s and 1880s. No president elected from 1876 through 1892 received a majority of the popular vote and Congress was usually closely divided between the parties. Each party had a strong incentive to find and recruit as many possible voters as they could. This produced a remarkably inclusive method of rousing voters for election: partisan mobilization. Each party extensively communicated with the entire electorate during the campaign season, unlike tightly targeted present-day campaign communication. It was rational for parties to pursue inclusive strategies back then, because the political technologies that permitted campaigns to identify and contact swing voters without contacting the entire electorate—polling and spot television and radio advertising—had yet to be invented. Faced with competitive elections and an inability to efficiently target communications, it made sense for the parties to contact everybody who might vote.

Jeremiah Jenks, a late–nineteenth-century political scientist, explained how party committees undertook widespread contact with voters:

> Before the election, arrangements are made by each local committee to canvass thoroughly the voters in the locality; to make a list containing all their names, with the parties to which they belong; to mention who are doubtful and, in consequence, are open to persuasion of any kind; and to give any other information regarding individual voters that will be of use in the coming election.... It is not too much to say that in important elections in doubtful states, every voter is individually looked after by local committees (Jenks 1896, 26–27).

In the closely fought presidential elections of the period, most states were "doubtful," leading parties to personally contact most voters during the campaign season.

Party contact worked well because party identification often overlapped with other well-established cleavages in America. It was a nation of homogeneous neighborhoods whose residents often shared a common faith, form of employment, newspaper, and party identification. In these neighborhoods, the favored local party contacted everyone at election time and provided governmental assistance and popular entertainment between elections. Party voting became a way of demonstrating community allegiance (Schier 2000, 60–61).

My great-grandfather, Stephen E. Schier (after whom I am named), is an example of how cultural and social ties reinforced party identification. Stephen grew up in the Mississippi River town of Fort Madison, Iowa, in the 1860s and 1870s and attended Catholic schools where instruction was in German. In Fort Madison, Catholics were Democrats and Protestants were Republicans. Stephen made a modest living working in a local haberdashery and read the local partisan paper, the *Evening Democrat*. His brother Henry won election when he ran as a Democrat for county sheriff. Stephen's vote for Grover Cleveland and the entire Democratic ticket in the 1884 election resulted from his membership in ethnic and religious communities and regular reading of the partisan press (Schier 2000, 60–61).

The major issue of the time—whether or not to keep and raise tariffs on imported manufactured goods—also supported party dominance of the political system. John J. Coleman (1996) identified four reasons why trade policy helped parties command government and politics in the 1870s and 1880s. First, control over tariffs lay with Congress, an institution dominated by parties. Second, trade issues directly affected the livelihoods of voters, making them central to elections. Raising tariffs raised the prices of imported goods for consumers; lower tariffs hurt domestic businesses. Third, opinions over the tariff tended to be stable during this period. Either one endorsed tariffs as an aid to local businesses or opposed them as a tax on consumers. Fourth, differences over the tariff overlapped with regional and ethnic divisions. Democrats, strong in the rural South and among immigrants, opposed higher tariffs as a tax on consumers. Republicans, favored by business and skilled workers, supported tariffs as an aid to business (12–21). Parties regularly squabbled over trade policy in elections and government, an issue conflict that helped to maintain the existing partisan divisions of the era.

America's partisan era of high turnout is particularly extraordinary in comparison with the politics of other nations at the time. No other democracy had as large an electorate. The United States provided universal voting for all males at that time, though rising racial discrimination increasingly restricted voting to white males after 1876. Male-only voting seems restrictive today, but few European nations were democracies at all in the 1870s, and those that were restricted the franchise to wealthy male citizens. The democratization of Europe in the late nineteenth and early twentieth centuries involved struggles to extend the franchise to all male citizens, a process completed in America by the 1870s (Lipset and Rokkan 1967). Not only was America's electorate comparatively large, it was extraordinarily active.

Sorting through the reasons for America's high-turnout era is complicated, but we need to identify them to understand why turnout dropped and how it might be resuscitated. Three major forces structured the politics of the period: the electoral competitiveness between the parties, the overlapping of partisan cleavages with social and cultural divisions in the country, and the opportune advent of the tariff issue. These forces made strong parties useful for politicians and voters. Once these incentives were in place, politicians used parties to structure an electoral system that maintained party dominance for decades.

They did so by strengthening state and local party organizations. State and local party organizations were much stronger than the national organizations at this time, reflecting the small size of national government and political stakes in national policy. America's national government was tiny by today's limited standards. In the late 1800s, national government expenditures equaled less than one-eighth of current levels. Beyond national trade issues, most matters of concern to voters were handled at the state and local levels. Most government jobs and laws were found there, as well. And it was state and local party organizations that structured the electoral system in a pro-party fashion.

Under party sway, elections operated in a fashion unheard of today. Until the late 1880s, nearly every state allowed parties to print up the ballots used on Election Day. Each prepared a "party strip" ballot with its own candidates listed on a single sheet of paper. Upon arriving at the polls, voters chose one of the two strip ballots and cast a straight-ticket vote most of the time. To split his ticket, a voter had to pick a party strip and write in or paste on the names of candidates other than those nominated by the parties. Party nominations involved closed processes dominated by local or state party leaders in which the party slate was agreed upon. Polling places were not staffed by public employees but by one representative from each of the two major parties. Elections occurred more often and for more offices than today, and the balloting seemed to never end. For example, in Ohio in the 1880s, voters had to select thirty county or state officials and those in larger cities had to choose fifteen more officeholders (Kornbluth 2000, 24). Frequent elections made party mobilization almost a constant activity, and the dizzying complexity of choices offered on Election Day made the simple party label a useful way for voters to negotiate the electoral maze.

Once in office, parties gained control of government jobs and services with which they could reward their loyal workers and voters. Parties also controlled the primary mass medium of the time—newspapers. Parties could direct their voters and advertising revenue to loyal papers, and all but a very few papers located in America's cities loyally touted a party message (Schudson 1978). Voters tended to receive news in a partisan fashion and gained social, material, and policy benefits by sticking with their party.

## Explaining Party Decline

Not everyone was thrilled with this strongly partisan electoral system. Though vote fraud was probably not that widespread (Allen and Allen 1981), enough revelations of dubious electoral activities appeared over the years to produce a strong political reform movement. As many as one in five New Jersey voters received cash for voting in the 1880s; Indiana politicians paid $15 a vote in 1888 (Schudson 1998, 163–64). Closely fought elections often ended amid charges of fraudulent ballots. At times, candidates purchased party nominations from party committees with cash (Schudson 1998, 152). Once in office, officials spread patronage jobs around to supporters, often regardless of qualifications, and engaged in "graft," padding public contracts in order to get a kickback from contractors (Riordan 1963).

The Progressive reform movement, dedicated to ending such practices, grew from elite segments of society. Committed to clean, efficient, and democratic government, middle- and upper-class professionals grew weary of party excesses and urged reforms to clean up the election system. They achieved increasing success during the first decades of the twentieth century. The reforms proved a major force for reducing voting turnout. An early change was the secret "Australian" ballot adopted by most states between 1887 and 1892 and by virtually all states by 1916 (Kornbluth 2000, 124–25). The parties at first welcomed the change because it would reduce the costs to them of ballot printing and staffing the polls, but the new system gave the government, not the parties, control over ballot structure and election administration. Eventually, Progressives used this governmental power to curb party authority.

One means of weakening party power was to make straight ticket voting more difficult. The private ballot made ticket splitting much easier, and further tinkering with ballot structure made party voting rarer. By 1917, most states had divided up the ballot into an "office block" format in which voters chose candidates for each office separately, or into a "party column" format that listed the candidates by party slate but required the voter to cast a ballot for each candidate individually. Only twelve states provided ballots by 1917 that allowed voters to cast a straight-ticket ballot by making a single mark at the top of the party column. Party emblems also were banned from ballots in more than two-thirds of the states, making it more difficult for voters new to the English language to cast a straight party ticket or vote at all (Kornbluth 2000, 125–26).

Reform of voter registration also curbed party power. Requiring registration for voting began early in the nineteenth century, but until the 1890s either local party officials were responsible for registering voters, or voters who registered themselves were registered to vote for life. Progressives found this loose system too susceptible to election fraud. By 1920, thirty-six states had adopted systems placing the responsibility for registration upon individual citizens, and the large majority of these states also required that citizens be regularly purged from the registration rolls if they had not voted in recent elections. Government officials, not party politicians, operated these new systems (Kornbluth 2000, 132–33). The system cut fraud but also reduced turnout by placing additional registration hurdles in front of voters. Elections also were scheduled less frequently, and the number of officials elected reduced. Many states placed local and state elections on different schedules than national elections. All this made it difficult for parties to maintain an ongoing mobilization of their voters.

Many southern states introduced literacy tests to curtail the African-American vote, but nine northern states also adopted them—an obvious attack on the immigrant supporters of party machines (Kornbluth 2000, 131–32). Progressives also spearheaded campaign finance reforms, and in 1907 reformers convinced Congress to ban corporate campaign contributions in federal elections. Federal laws also sought (unsuccessfully) to curb campaign spending, as did laws passed in many states. States outlawed Election Day cash payments, widespread during the partisan era. As parties lost funds, candidate-centered campaigns became more common (Troy 1991, 108–32).

A hallmark Progressive reform was the direct primary nomination of party candidates for office. Instead of nomination by party leaders in the celebrated "smoke-filled rooms" of the party era, voters would pick a nominee at the polls. Spearheaded by Robert M. LaFollette, Progressive governor of Wisconsin, by 1917 more than three-quarters of the states had adopted direct primaries for all statewide offices, and a majority of the states adopted presidential primaries (Kornbluth 2000, 127). Party organizations lost the ability to name their own candidates for office, greatly reducing their power in electoral politics. America remains the only major democracy in the world that has primary nominations.

Similar participatory reforms adopted by many states involved the initiative, referendum, and recall. These laws sought to curtail the power of the often party-dominated state legislatures. By 1917, twenty-two states had adopted initiative and referendum systems allowing voters to bypass legislative bodies and vote directly on legislation. Recall, in which voters can eject an incumbent from office in the middle of her term through a popular vote, had become law in eleven states (Kornbluth 2000, 128–29). Patronage employment also began to disappear, and by 1912 was almost completely gone from the federal government and most state governments, due to the adoption of the civil-service principles of merit employment. Substantive competence replaced party connections in securing government jobs. Progressives also successfully championed the growth of regulatory boards and commissions charged with regulating business and labor. These bipartisan or nonpartisan bodies, appointed by political executives, addressed controversial policy areas that parties and legislatures had often sought to avoid (Schier 2000, 70).

Concurrent with Progressive reforms came two other trends that shrank party power. By the turn of the century, major independent newspapers had arisen in many large American cities, reducing the ability of parties to dominate political communication. Parties became less able to fund newspapers and independent, often sensational "yellow" journalism with more limited political content found a ready audience in metropolitan centers. In addition, interest groups began to grow in number and influence in the early twentieth century. New issues that the parties were reluctant to handle—consumer protection, regulation of business, or social welfare—found advocates through the formation of independent groups. The stable politics of the late nineteenth century, based heavily on trade policy, gave way to a more complicated politics resulting from the problems of industrialization (Schier 2000, 68–76).

Progressive reforms made government more complex and difficult for citizens to understand, and made voting more costly for many of them. Individual citizens had the responsibility for registration, and casting a ballot was a far more complicated undertaking than before. The material benefits of voting for a particular party also largely vanished. Government became less a matter of two parties than of a flurry of individual politicians, interest groups, and bureaucrats in constant and confusing interaction. In short, the roots of our contemporary electoral system and its many problems lie in the Progressive reforms. What impact did the reforms have on turnout? The record is mixed, with some (Converse 1974; Rusk 1970, 1974) claiming large negative impacts on participation from certain reforms and others (Kleppner 1982; Burnham 1965) finding small declines in voting resulting from them. The voting environment became much more forbidding to many voters. As Alan Kornbluth (2000) puts it: "Electoral reforms can best be understood as permissive rather than determinative factors.... Reformers capitalized on a rapidly degenerating system of mass-based partisan politics and sped the process along" (136–37).

The Progressive reforms, in addition to reducing turnout, lessened the ability of America's electoral system to promote accountability, deliberation, and stability. More complicated voting procedures and fewer party-based elections made holding elected officials accountable more difficult for many voters. Party-centered deliberation in government would eventually be replaced by a constant responsiveness to organized interest groups by politicians operating as independent political entrepreneurs. Parties can provide a shield for officeholders from "special interests," but they lost much of that capacity early in the twentieth century. The political stability of the electoral system remains at long-term risk because of the falling turnouts fostered in part by the Progressive reforms.

The decay of political parties and declining turnout in the early twentieth century were prompted by more than the Progressive movement's successes. A second major force lowering turnout operated concurrently with the reforms. Electoral politics became much less competitive in many regions of the country because of the 1896 election (Kornbluth 2000, 139–40). It was a "realigning election" in which the party identifications of many groups in the electorate shifted for the long term (Burnham 1970, 11–34). The Democrats in 1896 offered presidential candidate William Jennings Bryan with his appeal for a weaker currency through a silver standard. The election solidified their hold on the South and West, rural areas with many debtors who would benefit from monetary devaluation. Republicans successfully dominated the more populous states by favoring a tougher monetary standard based on gold that would stabilize the industrial economy. The South became a region dominated by the Democratic Party, with Republicans preeminent in the Midwest and Northeast and in national politics as a whole. Republicans held the presidency for all but four years from 1896 to 1932, and usually dominated Congress as well.

The decline in party competitiveness made more elections foregone conclusions and lessened the need for the dominant party in a particular region to maximize turnout. It is simply more efficient to win cheaply by avoiding full-scale mobilization when your party is likely to prevail anyway. Paul Kleppner's quantitative analysis of the turnout decline after 1896 found that ebbing electoral competition accounted for one-quarter to one-third of the drop in turnout after 1896 (Kleppner 1982, 184).

Turnout did drop for a short period in the early 1920s after women got the right to vote (through the Nineteenth Amendment of 1920), but that decline was small compared to the drop-off that occurred before 1920. In the few states that permitted female voting before 1920, turnout declined after 1900 as it had in other states (Kornbluth 2000, 105–7). Finally, although African Americans were excluded throughout the South—through such obstacles as literacy tests—fewer than half of southern whites voted from 1900 to 1910 (Kousser 1974, 26). Thus we are left with Progressive reforms and declining interparty competition as the shaping forces producing the first era of sharply declining turnout.

## ANOTHER DIP IN VOTING: 1968–2000

Turnout rose in the 1930s, however, as economically stressed Americans sought governmental solutions to the Great Depression. Turnout in the 1936 presidential election was 5.1 percent above that of 1928 (61 percent compared to 56.9 percent), but well below the "total turnout" levels of the 1880s. From the 1930s into the 1960s, about 60 percent of the voting age population turned out for presidential elections and 44 to 49 percent turned out in off-year congressional elections. Then, turnout slumped again. Presidential voting has only reached 60 percent once since 1968, and congressional turnouts usually remained below 40 percent of the voting age population. What prompted this second long-term downturn in turnout?

The drop-off is initially puzzling, because a "chief factor affecting the costs of voting in the United States," the voter registration system, has become much less restrictive since 1960 (Texeira 1992, 29). Literacy tests and poll taxes, in place in several states in 1960, are now gone. More states allow registration by mail, bilingual election materials are available, dates for closing registration rolls have moved closer to Election Day, and state residency requirements for voting have been reduced. In addition, in the 1990s the Motor Voter reform became law, allowing citizens to register when they renewed their driver's licenses. Voters are also more educated, far more than in the 1880s, which presumably increases the electorate's understanding of elections. All this lowers the costs of voting, and should have boosted turnout. But it did not. Why?

Ruy Texeira's (1992) analysis of turnout decline identifies a decline in "social connectedness" and a public withdrawal from the political world as reasons for turnout decline (49). The electorate became younger and less well integrated into their communities. Further, the public came to view government as less responsive or important in satisfying their needs (49; Nye, Zelikow, and King 1997). Texeira also argues that the declining ability of parties to mobilize voters and more complex election calendars also probably contributed to the decline (Texeira 1992, 53–59). In all, it was less due to rising costs than to a perception of decreased benefits from political participation.

So why did people perceive fewer benefits from voting and political participation?

The turbulent issues of the 1960s and 1970s increased levels of political alienation and shrank the benefits of voting for many citizens. A major scholarly analysis of declining trust in government identifies the political controversies of that era as a major why public confidence in government plummeted (Nye, Zelikow, and King 1997, conclusion). Concurrently, partisan identification among the public decreased and the number of self-identified independents rose. "The issues that loosened party ties were racial conflict and Vietnam, capped off with Watergate. These issues caused substantial discontent. They led the public to turn against the political parties and the political process more generally" (Nie, Verba, and Petrocik 1976, 350). Along with the number of political independents, the incidence of split-ticket voting also rose in the last quarter of the twentieth century.

Such behavior extended well beyond the period in which it arose, suggesting that other long-term factors made voting seem less worthwhile to many Americans. Much of that lingering perception lies in the changing nature of the way parties, interests, and candidates approach voters during election campaigns. Specifically, it is the difference between contemporary campaign activation and traditional partisan mobilization. First, the two processes differ in their *focus*. Mobilization was inclusive, and practically everybody voted during the partisan era. Modern activation is exclusive by design. Candidates, parties, and interests identify those parts of the public most likely to participate politically on their behalf and employ a variety of methods to induce their activism. This allows political elites to spend millions of dollars efficiently, speaking to only a few citizens.

Mobilization and activation also differ in their *agents,* or sources of stimulation. Strong party organizations dominated the mobilization process and most voters thought of politics primarily in terms of parties. No more. Now a bevy of interest groups contacts the public about political issues, and elections feature a multitude of candidates campaigning on the basis of personal appeal. Political communication grows blurry for most voters. Mobilization also involved *methods* different from activation. Moving people to vote by party proved effective when the partisan message was delivered by personal contact and local newspapers (the main means of political communication 120 years ago). Activation uses more focused techniques. Television advertisements, telephone calls, direct mail, and Internet communications are carefully aimed at a specific group of citizens.

Most important, mobilization and activation have different effects on the American electoral system. Mobilization produced heavy turnouts and allowed voters to cast clear and decisive party ballots in potentially confusing elections. By electing party teams, it became easier to hold government accountable. High turnouts helped the political stability of the electoral system and encouraged deliberation over policy within party councils. Activation hardly ensures that elected officials are accountable to the mass of citizens. The confusing profusion of candidates and election advertisements makes voting an information burden, reducing turnout. Governmental deliberation becomes less possible when officeholders are constantly "running scared." Activation also spurs the rise of popular alienation, identified by Texeira as a major reason for declining turnout. The benefits of voting become obscure to many voters in such a system, because activation "works to further the purposes of particular political elites during elections and when they lobby government, regardless of what most citizens think or desire. It is now possible for candidates, parties and interests to rule without serious regard for majority preferences expressed in the polling booth" (Schier 2000, 9).

A closer look at the biases of contemporary campaign activation fleshes out the above generalizations. Empirical research consistently shows that campaigns aim their messages at voters who are disproportionately well educated. They "target people who are likely to respond to and be effective.

They target the educated, the wealthy and the powerful" (Rosenstone and Hansen 1993, 241). These same people have disproportionate influence over governmental actions. Minorities actively engaged in current issues— "attentive publics"—are particularly important in the politics of activation (Arnold 1990, 60–68). Their power lies in an ability to get the message out to less attentive citizens about what government is doing. This causes much of officeholders' deliberation to be responsive to small parts of the public that can threaten incumbents with adverse publicity. So many interest groups have learned the art of activating an attentive public that government is swamped with a cacophony of demands. Groups "begin to choke the system that bred them, to undermine confidence in politics. . . . The system might begin to defeat the purpose for which it exists, namely to make reasonable social decisions quickly" (Rauch 1994, 61). This results in the decay of governmental deliberation: "the number and diversity of interests have increased without any corresponding increase in the strength of the process for integrating interests; and plebiscitary techniques have gained ground without a corresponding increase in representativeness and deliberation" (Dahl 1994, 38).

It is little wonder that many citizens do not see the use of voting in such a convoluted system. There are many political messages heard during campaigns, but they are aimed at a strategically selected few. Citizens often encounter a lot of noise during an election but find that very little of it speaks to their personal concerns as a citizen and voter. In the polling booth, one chooses among candidates, each of whom relies heavily on political activists and interests for election, who run individualistic campaigns that sell themselves. In addition, these interest groups, continually activating small parts of the public to press the government with grievances, can have disproportionate influence over public policy. Will all of the "individualistic" officeholders, so vulnerable to political pressures given the constant need to worry about reelection, be able to fashion coherent policy? And if they do or do not, will it be clear whom to hold accountable? Our profoundly antiparty electoral system makes that task difficult. Voters thus view voting as offering fewer benefits, prompting America's recent trend of lower turnouts.

## VOICES OF NONVOTERS

Exploring the views of America's nonvoters gives some clues as to their reasons for electoral inaction. Low education seems an unlikely explanation for their nonvoting, because a recent survey discovered that 80 percent of nonvoters had at least a high school education (Doppelt and Shearer 1999, 231). They do, however, evidence distrust in the political system, with 64 percent agreeing that "most elected officials do not care what people like me think" (224). In interviews, few of them demonstrated any clear understanding of ideology or partisanship. Consistent with Neuman's research revealing low public sophistication about politics, few of them mentioned or reliably defined the terms "liberal," "conservative," "Democrat," or "Republican." Instead, they discussed politics almost entirely in terms of individual personalities—particularly those of recent presidents—and their immediate personal experiences. As one interviewee put it, the news she cared about most was what was happening in her neighborhood (119).

Despite their limited exposure to political substance, nonvoters reacted quite negatively to contemporary politics. One recalled the "negative and ugly" political advertisements from the 1996 U.S. Senate race in Georgia (Doppelt and Shearer 1999, 103). Several decried the importance of money in elections and the importance of "special interest groups" in elections and governing (60, 103, 128). Another saw no need to vote because "the system will continue to ignore average people no matter who's elected" (84). None saw any real reward for voting, regardless of the cost of going to the polls.

Nonvoters' perceptions are a natural consequence of the politics of activation. The political system, they believe, does not speak to them or their needs. Electoral messages seldom address nonvoters. Activation politics often generates nasty television advertisements and features a horde of interest groups seeking particular benefits from government. Candidates, parties, and interests find little incentive to inform nonvoters of the benefits of casting their ballots. They return the favor by staying home on Election Day.

## And Elsewhere?

The size of the gap in turnout between the United States and other stable democracies is large—an average of 20 percent from the average of other systems and over 35 percent from Austria, Australia, and Belgium, nations with very high turnouts (Texeira 1992, 7–8; see Table 3.1). Those three countries have made voting mandatory by national law, raising the costs of nonvoting enough to propel practically all citizens to the polls. In contrast, America's registration system raises the costs of voting. The large majority of stable democracies make voter registration the responsibility of government; only in the United States and France is it the task of individual citizens. Universal registration stimulates high turnouts, which in turn encourages parties to target less and generate more inclusive messages that maintain high turnout. It is, compared to America's exclusive politics, a virtuous cycle.

Other nations also lower the costs of voting by having less frequent elections. Robert Jackman and Ross Miller (1995), in a study of turnout in twenty democracies, found that the frequency of elections depressed turnout, controlling for other social, cultural, and electoral structure variables. They concluded "the distinctly high volume of elections" in America "depresses turnout by encouraging voter fatigue" (483). Elections in other democracies are much more party-based than in America, which also lowers costs to voters by reducing the information required to cast a ballot consistent with one's issue or accountability preferences. In America, thanks to our confusing politics of activation, voters must stock up information on all sorts of individualistic candidates. This is unnecessary in Germany, Great Britain, New Zealand, Canada, Italy, Belgium, Sweden, France, or most other long-established democracies.

The key benefits that electoral systems can provide to voters are "the importance of the electoral contest" or *electoral salience*—"the likelihood that one's vote will not be wasted" through allocating electoral results proportionately (Franklin 1996, 231–32). The above summary of nonvoters' attitudes shows how electoral salience is remarkably low among many citizens. Given that elections are complex, confusing, frequently nasty in their advertising tone, and narrowly targeted at small parts of the public, it is hardly surprising that so many Americans find them unimportant. Nonproportional election results also shrink the benefits of voting. America's single-member plurality system ensures that many votes will be wasted in noncompetitive single-member district elections and winner-take-all allocations of electoral votes in presidential contests. It is little wonder that American turnout is low, once we examine the practices of other electoral systems.

Party decline and Progressive reforms loom large in any comprehensive explanation of low American turnout. Party-based elections make electoral politics more understandable to more voters and permissive registration systems boost voting by lowering the barriers to the polling booth. In the Progressive era, Americans decisively turned away from both of these features, opening the way for an era of exclusive activation featuring candidate-centered campaigns. America's long-standing embrace of SMP systems also means that many votes that are cast just do not matter. Raising turnout depends upon rebuilding our electoral system on the principles of party-based elections and universal registration. America also should employ electoral arrangements that reduce the number of wasted votes. These reforms will raise turnout, enhance the legitimacy and political stability of the political system, make it easier for voters to hold party "governing teams" accountable, and restore party-based deliberation to government.

## So What?

Despite the growth in hostility to government in recent decades, the republic seems secure, with little obvious threat to its core institutions. Given this, why is low turnout a problem? Some nonvoters, like Gene Tencza, are, after all "pretty happy with the way it is" (Doppelt and Shearer 1999, 79). One could argue, then, that low turnout is not a sign of public disaffection, but rather one of public satisfaction. Because nothing is terribly wrong, by this logic, many people do not vote because they are not disturbed enough to do so. Low turnout becomes evidence of the health of the political system.

This is a dubious argument. By its logic, America's electoral system is healthier than is practically any other in the world. That is true only if nonvoting is a sign of contentment, and we have much evidence that it is not. Numerous surveys have charted the rise in political alienation and distrust in recent decades, attitudes particularly strong among nonvoters. Consider the views of Michael Keegan, representative of many nonvoters interviewed by Doppelt and Shearer: "I've never been in a voting booth, but I'm saying something by not voting.... Everybody in politics has lost the reality that the public wants to hear the truth and not bull.... Give me somebody to vote for and I'll vote" (Doppelt and Shearer 1999, 148).

A subtler defense of nonvoting comes from political scientists Bernard Berelson, Paul Lazarsfeld, and William McPhee (1999). Admitting that many Americans fall short of the requirements for sound citizenship, such as adequate political knowledge and regular voting, they view the American public's variable participation levels as important for maintaining regime stability. "For political democracy to survive ... the intensity of conflict must be limited, the rate of change must be restrained" (209). A stable democracy requires some to be quite active and some to be less active.

> Lack of interest by some people is not without its benefits, too. . . . Extreme interest goes with extreme partisanship and might culminate in rigid fanaticism that could destroy democratic processes if generalized throughout the community. Low interest provides maneuvering room for political shifts necessary for a complex society in a period of rapid change. Some people are and should be highly interested in politics, but not everyone is or needs to be. Only the doctrinaire would deprecate the modern indifference that facilitates compromise (Berelson, Lazarsfeld, and McPhee 1999, 210)

It is true that societies convulsed by intense divisions are often both unstable and characterized by high voting turnouts. The German election of 1933 that elevated Adolf Hitler to the chancellorship had high turnout. However, most major democracies today have high turnouts and no such wrenching divisions. The contemporary United States is far from the threat of dire divisions raised by Berelson and his colleagues. The threat to our stability instead stems from low participation. "As fewer and fewer citizens participate, the extent to which government truly rests on the consent of the governed may be called into question," resulting in "gridlocked government and a political culture that devalues government and turns talented people away from careers in public service" (Texeira 1992, 101–2). Much of this vicious cycle exists at present. Politics becomes abhorrent to more citizens, reducing the talent pool in politics, and, over the long term, the legitimacy of the electoral and governmental system itself. The threat to political stability comes from turnout that is too low in America, not too high.[2]

Low turnout also weakens the accountability of American government. Political elites are the "critical element for the health of a democratic order" (Key 1961, 64) and elections are the primary way that the mass public can hold them accountable for their actions. "Participation in elections . . . should ideally function as a democratic counterweight to high impact, resource intensive activism, exposing elites to signals from a relatively wide array of needs and interests. When nonvoting is widespread, however—and is also significantly class skewed [as it is in the United States]—participation in elections may fail to play that role effectively" (Texeira 1992, 103). Because most citizens do not pay close attention to politics, accountability requires that the electoral system make their voting duties simple and manageable. American voting procedures are so bulky and unmanageable that they impede the public's ability to check the elites that, through their mastery of activation politics, now dominate the councils of government. Interest groups and political activists currently prosper at mass expense, thanks to nonvoting. This "division of labor" impedes popular control of American government.

Though low turnout persists as a shortcoming of American elections, voguish reforms of recent years propose still more choices for voters. The participatory reforms of initiative, referendum, and recall have spread to more states, and there have been calls for adoption of these procedures by the national government. The next chapter reveals how the initiative process actually weakens the ability of citizens to hold government accountable. It also curbs the motivation and opportunity for elected officials to work through the details of policy once in office.

CHAPTER 4

# Direct Democracy or Legislative Government?

It is the latest fashion, and all sorts of people crave it. Direct democracy—initiative, referendum, and recall—is the hot new vogue in America's electoral system. Adopted at the state and local levels, these mechanisms allow the public to directly make policy or abruptly end an elected official's term. The *initiative* is a procedure by which citizen petitions can place proposals for changes in state law or state constitutions directly on the ballot for a public vote. Twenty-four states allow citizens to propose legal or constitutional changes for voter approval in this way. A *statutory referendum* allows citizens to vote on laws considered by the state legislature. Two sorts of statutory referendum processes are used among the twenty-six states that employ them. One variant, the *legislative referral*, permits the legislature to put a potential law to a popular vote. If the voters approve, it becomes law. A second type, the *popular referendum,* enables citizens—if they gather enough signatures on a petition—to force a public vote on a recently enacted law (Ellis 2002, 3–4). A *constitutional referendum,* employed in every state but Alabama, requires a public vote on proposed amendments to the state's constitution. A *recall* law, adopted in twenty states and many municipalities, allows citizens by petition to require a recall election on whether an elected official should complete her/his term of office. Though other democratic nations at times employ national referenda, none use direct democracy on a scale approaching that of some American states, such as California and Oregon. Table 4.1 summarizes the characteristics of initiative, referendum, and recall.

The initiative process now receives the heaviest usage in its history and is extremely popular with the public. In 1996, the ninety-three initiatives that appeared on ballots marked the highest usage of the initiative ever, followed closely by the eighty-five initiatives in 2000. Many controversial issues have landed on the initiative ballot in recent years—gay rights, anti-affirmative action, term limits, school vouchers, legalization of marijuana, tax cuts, and campaign finance reform. A survey by Rasmussen Research in 1998 found that 64 percent of Americans agreed that it was a good idea for states to adopt the initiative process, whereas 17 percent disagreed (Broder 2000, 229). Moreover, almost two-thirds of Americans favor the creation of a national initiative process (Broder 2000, 229).

Political elites also find initiatives useful for their own ends, which have little to do with unleashing the democratic voice of the people. David Magleby, a leading analyst of the initiative process, explains why: "The media love it, because it's easy to report. The politicians love it, because they can use it to advance their careers. The interest groups love it, because their dollars can buy more in the way of policy results than any other

TABLE 4.1  Types of Direct Democracy and Their Frequency in the States

| Type | Process | Frequency |
| --- | --- | --- |
| Statutory Initiative | Citizens have the right to propose new state laws and pass them through a popular vote | 21 states |
| Constitutional Initiative | Citizens have the right to propose amendments to the state's constitution and pass them through a popular vote | 17 states |
| Statutory Referendum | Citizens have the right to petition for a vote on laws passed by the state legislature or the legislature can refer potential laws to citizens for a referendum vote | 26 states |
| Constitutional Referendum | Citizens have the right to vote on proposed amendments to their state's Constitution | 49 states |
| Recall | Citizens have the right via petition to call a special election on whether to immediately end the term of an elected official holding state or local office | 20 states |

*Source*: Howard R. Ernst, "The Historical Role of Narrow-Material Interests in Initiative Politics," in *Dangerous Democracy? The Ballot over Ballot Initiatives in America,* ed. Larry J. Sabato, Howard R. Ernst, and Bruce A. Larson (Lanham, Md.: Rowman and Littlefield, 2001), 2–5.

expenditure. And the political consultants love it because, as one of them told me, 'Absent personalities, tactics prevail'" (quoted in Broder 2000, 235). Though the public loves the democratic prospect of the initiative process, political elites find it quite useful for their own purposes. Moreover, those purposes do not necessarily involve facilitating majority rule, just activating enough of the public to satisfy elite agendas (Schier 2000, 141–54). We need to examine the reality behind the venerable arguments in favor of direct democracy.

Consider the impact of initiative, referendum, and recall procedures upon the accountability, deliberation, voting turnout, and stability of the American political system. The initiative promises accountability by allowing the public to make laws directly, essentially making the public accountable to themselves. However, the reality behind this beguiling generalization is unsettling. Who puts issues on the ballot? That is a great agenda setting power. Are these agenda setters accountable to the public? By definition, the initiative dispenses with legislative deliberation over policy, allowing the voters to reflect over it if they wish before they cast their ballots. And the choice is up or down, with no possibility of amendment. As Bruce Cain and Kenneth Miller (2001) put it, the initiative process undermines "opportunities for refinement, informed deliberation, consensus building and compromise" (43). Further, the political manipulation of agenda control and strategic voting often makes it impossible for coherent public verdicts to reliably result from such elections, further impeding accountability (Riker 1982). Ballot initiatives seem to have little effect on turnout, though a ballot weighed down by several initiatives may encourage voters to stop voting after a few choices are registered (Cronin 1989, 226–28). In fact, the drop-off rate is 5 to 15 percent in state issue elections (Cronin 1989, 67, 227). The initiative's impact on stability and legitimacy is more complex. It may increase governmental legitimacy overall because of its popularity, but it does limit and constrain state legislatures from making policy, injecting uncertainty into their deliberations and increasing political and policymaking instability.

The referendum produces far less extensive impacts on state electoral systems. The effects on turnout, as with the initiative, seem minimal, though ballots that are more complex do contribute to voter drop-off. Referenda do not eclipse legislative deliberation, but are rather the consequence of it. Because legislatures determine what goes on the ballot, referenda operate more as an incremental popular check on legislative deliberation than a wholesale replacement of it, as is the initiative. Referenda also challenge the stability of legislative government far less than do initiatives because referenda are the products of representative government. Referenda do potentially allow the public to hold legislatures accountable on issues. However, given the distortions of agenda control and strategic voting in such elections, they may not reliably produce that sort of accountability (Riker 1982), particularly given the information demands they make upon an inattentive electorate.

The recall provides accountability much more securely than does either the initiative or referendum. Recalls are much more consistent with liberal democracy or republicanism, which requires that "voting permits the rejection of candidates or officials who have offended so many voters that they cannot win an election" (Riker 1982, 242). Though it is a Progressive reform and involves a direct democratic mechanism, the recall allows a form of candidate-centered accountability that voters can successfully execute, which probably explains the high turnouts in special recall elections (Cronin 1989, 143). Still, recalls are one more addition to an overcrowded election schedule that wears out voters and keeps turnouts overall low. Political stability and deliberation, however, can suffer through use of recall elections. They can undermine the ability of legislators to "refine and enlarge" policy through deliberation because of the fear they strike into lawmakers who already are running scared. Recalls can keep lawmakers on such short leashes that they cower from the prospect of employing the independent judgment that is vital to legislative deliberation. Moreover, recall elections, though popular and thus contributing to political system legitimacy, can disrupt governmental stability. Governmental officials consumed with recall elections are inevitably distracted from their duties. Other means remain for removing miscreant elected officials: impeachment, criminal prosecution, and voluntary resignation.

In sum, the referendum disturbs the liberal democracy of Madisonian republicanism little, the recall somewhat, and the initiative a great deal. The rest of this chapter focuses on the initiative because of the challenge it presents to governmental accountability, deliberation, and stability. We begin by exploring the beginnings of these three participatory reforms and the arguments for them.

## THE DEVELOPMENT OF DIRECT DEMOCRACY

Though initiative, referendum, and recall are commonly labeled Progressive reforms, their origins reach back before the Progressive movement.

Use of the recall reaches back to ancient Athens and the Roman republic, and was resurrected by critics of the corrupt, party-dominated politics of the late nineteenth century. The first outspoken proponents of these direct democracy reforms were leaders of the Populist movement of the 1890s. Populists arose from the ranks of financially strapped farmers to argue against what they viewed as the oppressive economic and political institutions of the time. The 1892 Populist Party platform called for adoption of the initiative and referendum. Populists saw direct democracy as a means of toppling the authority of legislatures corruptly dominated, in their view, by corporate interests. Direct rule by the people became the dominant issue for many populists (Hicks 1931, 406–7). They trusted the public to govern wisely and well when entrusted with direct democracy.

The first five states to adopt the initiative were in the West where populism was strong—South Dakota (the first in 1898), Utah, Oregon, Montana, and Oklahoma (by 1907). The initiative and referendum became widespread in the following decade, the apex of the Progressive movement. By 1918, nineteen states had the initiative and twenty-two the referendum (Ernst 2001, 11). Progressives were a broad coalition of reformers, many highly educated, who placed less emphasis on economic issues and direct democracy than did the Populists. The goal of Progressivism was less direct rule by the people than clean, efficient government through the overthrow of party rule. Party leaders of the time indulged in graft and influence peddling in state and local governments, and the Progressives meant to stop that. Instead of challenging the basic structure of the economic system, as did many more radical Populists, Progressives wanted to clean up the economic and political system through governmental regulation and procedural reform. "Unlike Populists, Progressives did not intend for their reforms (including the initiative) to undermine representative government; instead, Progressives wanted to redeem and strengthen government" (Cain and Miller 2001, 36).

The initiative gained widespread use immediately upon its adoption in many states, but after this initial burst of activity, it was used less frequently. The next great wave of initiative use is currently upon us, beginning in 1978 with the passage of Proposition 13 in California, a dramatic measure that placed a rollback of the property tax into the state constitution. Several reasons lay behind the upsurge in initiatives. Growing public alienation from politics and governmental institutions probably made direct rule through initiatives more appealing. The big growth in organized interests since the 1960s led many of them to pursue their policy goals through initiatives. In addition, an "initiative industrial complex" of lawyers, pollsters, and political consultants sprang up to encourage and maintain the business of getting proposals qualified for initiatives and conducting campaigns. This mature industry thrives by keeping initiative votes before the public.

## THE INITIATIVE BUSINESS

The initiative industry exists because getting an issue on the ballot is not a simple process. To prevent ballot overload, the entryway to the initiative process is narrow. Activists and interest organizations have to mobilize money and technical expertise to put their issue before voters. The process is a lengthy one and is not for political amateurs. Todd Donovan, Shaun Bowler, and David McCuan (2001), in a recent analysis of the "initiative industrial complex," explained the elaborate procedures for qualifying an issue for the ballot (102–23).

Step one involves deciding on the issue and the strategy for pursuing it. Lawyers who specialize in political law must draft the proposal's ballot language. Even at this early point in the process, the professional advocates from organized interests differ from the more spontaneous amateur advocates who spring up around an issue. Amateurs seldom get beyond this initial talking stage, because of the financial and time burdens necessary to get initiatives on the ballot. Interest group professionals dominate the initiative process now. Initiative proponents expend funds to employ expert drafting help and begin immediately consulting with hired political consultants about the proposed initiative. An initiative professional called California's 1978 Proposition 13 "the last amateur campaign" to succeed in that it did not have heavy interest group funding or involve professional consultants (McCuan et al. 1998, 73). One consultant indicated he read proposals after they were written, "to make sure there is nothing politically incorrect in there, or something that will really bite you" (Zimmerman 1997, 1).

Opinion research by initiative proponents comes next. Again, more "professional" organized interests, be they labor unions, businesses, or "issue" groups such as environmentalists or "good government" groups like Common Cause, are much more likely to have the funds to research how to best sell their issue to the public. The research process usually operates in the following sequence. First, consultants employ "focus groups," a common technique in commercial marketing, in which a group of twelve to twenty citizens discusses with a trained moderator several open-ended questions about the initiative's topic. From these sessions, consultants discover which arguments seem particularly persuasive to citizens who know little about the issue and/or are undecided about it. Next, random-sample opinion polls test the efficacy of various arguments, so that future advertisements will present the most convincing case. "Polling takes the language, opinions and arguments raised by the focus groups and tests them with a random sampling of state voters," in the words of one initiative activist (Schultz 1996, 16).

The poll and focus group findings help the proponents to phrase the issue to maximum advantage. William Riker (1986) labels this a "manipulation of dimensions" of the issue, showing the one aspect of a complex choice that most helps its advocates. It is a form of manipulation, like agenda control and strategic voting, that renders a coherent public judgment on initiatives impossible because voters received limited, manipulated information. In 1998, Californians voted on Proposition 226, a proposal to bar trade unions from automatically taking a portion of their members' dues and using them for partisan political activities. Proponents ran advertisements emphasizing corrupt labor bosses. Opponents ran equally sensational advertisements arguing its passage would cause sweatshops to blossom and jobs to fly overseas (Broder 2000, 104–46). The rivals each put their best spin on the issue, highlighting only a few aspects of a complex proposal. Voters cannot be blamed for failing to grasp those complexities. However, as Riker (1982) notes, such an outcome hardly produces an issue mandate. Mandates come from deliberation, not manipulation, and deliberation is curiously absent from initiative politics.

The following steps in the process flow from the research and strategic choices made at the drafting stage. Issue proponents try to build coalitions of likeminded activists and organizations for the oncoming campaign. Negotiations can take months or years as each organization tries to get its concerns satisfied in initiative language and campaign strategy. When the advocates agree on their language and strategy, they then approach state officials to work out the official title and ballot summary. This is a tricky process of negotiation. Advocates try to get the most persuasive ballot language and summary they can. It may involve redrafting by the proponents. Their goal is language with maximum manipulative ability. After the language becomes official, proponents seek endorsements, and they are important. In many initiative states, the official initiative voter guide from the state government will list endorsing organizations and often such groups can put in statements of support for the initiative. Voters frequently mention the state guides as important sources of information on initiatives (Donovan, Bowler, and McCuan 2001, 109–10).

No initiative can appear on a state ballot unless enough citizens sign official petitions requesting a ballot placement. State regulations for this vary, but they usually require a percentage of the state's registered voters or of votes cast in the last statewide election. The requirement usually amounts to several hundred thousand signatures. Though sometimes advocates accomplish this solely with volunteers, the common method now entails hiring professional signature-gathering firms to supplement volunteer efforts or to collect the lion's share of needed signatures. Firms charge between $0.50 and $2.00 per signature, so the cost for raising the signatures easily escalates into hundreds of thousands of dollars for a single initiative. This cost limits the initiative agenda to issues whose advocates have many activist volunteers, vast funds, or both.

The petition drive thus becomes an important battlefield involving activists and organized interests. Opponents of proposed initiatives find this an important choke point. One political consultant described the strategy: "You hire a consultant early on to monitor and sometimes even run a counter campaign so people will not sign an initiative. Sometimes you will hire a consultant after an initiative qualifies, but in California and big-time elections, especially where big interest groups are attacked … opponents start in early before an initiative qualifies" (quoted in Dash [1997] 2001, 1).

A critical concern for initiative proponents is the official description of the proposition included in the guide sent to all state voters. Guides usually include an official summary of the proposition, followed by supporting and dissenting views from various interest groups. Proponents focus on influencing the official language and sometimes have success, given the limits of state officials' expertise. As one Colorado official admitted: "I write the pros and cons that go into the official state booklet and I also work for the state legislature [deputy director, Legislative Counsel's office], but, in all honesty, I sometimes don't know what's the guts of an issue; that is, what the consequences of it would be if the voters passed it" (quoted in Cronin 1989, 80). The more initiatives in a state, the more verbiage in its voter guide. The 1996 Oregon booklet totaled 248 pages. Secretary of State Phil Kiesling described it as "almost as long as *War and Peace,* but with less of a discernable plot" (Broder 2000, 207). It is unlikely that most voters study them carefully. California political scientist John Allswang assessed a recent state voter guide: "the average American doesn't read that much serious nonfiction in a year" (quoted in Jones 2001, 224). The less voters and officials understand, the more opportunity initiative activists have for manipulation.

Opponents often try to cloud the issue by offering "counter-initiatives." Multiple incentives make this an inviting option. Counter-initiatives can contain language voiding the original initiative if both get a majority vote from the state's voters. A well-funded opponent can pay top dollar for signatures to a counterinitiative, bidding up costs for proponents of the original initiative. Moreover, if the opponent's issue qualifies, proponents of the original initiative may have to divert funds to fight it, draining them of the ability to sell their original proposal. In addition, in big states like California, it is cheaper to qualify a counter-initiative than to conduct a full-fledged campaign against an initiative. Finally, studies find the longer the ballot, the more likely voters will vote against initiatives (Donovan, Bowler, and McCuan 2001, 123).

The tendency of voters to reject initiatives they do not understand is the basis for all strategies in the initiative campaigns that follow ballot qualification. If adequately funded, an opposition campaign can succeed just by sewing doubts via radio and election advertisements, direct mailings, telephone calls, and personal contact with voters. Dawn Laugens, a consultant and veteran of initiative campaigns in California, Ohio, Maine, and other states, describes the strategies in play:

> The key is to make the abstraction real for voters. That means you have to understand your audience and segment your message to reach each important part of it. Usually, the proponents have described the objective of the measure in positive, appealing terms. To persuade them to vote no, you have to go after competing values—create conflict in their minds. You tell them the initiative is flawed. It will have unintended consequences. The people behind it are bad. Anything that causes them to reconsider (quoted in Broder 2000, 114).

Initiatives involve the targeted activation of likely voters by well-financed interests. They differ from contemporary candidate elections only in that voters vote on language, not people. It is an expensive business. In 1997–98, total spending for and against statewide initiatives was $257,053,852 in the initiative states, with California alone accounting for $141,274,345 of that total (Broder 2000, 163–64). The price of admission to initiative politics is steep: "Without money ... the money of self-interested politicians and political parties, or of insurance companies, or of Silicon Valley millionaires, or labor unions—initiative proponents can't get to the table at all" (Schrag 2001, 253). Unlike candidate campaigns, direct spending by interests and wealthy individuals is totally unlimited.

The U.S. Supreme Court upheld the role of unlimited money in initiative politics in *First National Bank of Boston v. Bellotti* (1978). The case involved a Massachusetts law prohibiting corporate expenditures on ballot proposals about "taxation of income." The court ruled that limitations on initiative spending by corporations constituted "an impermissible legislative prohibition of speech based on the identity of the interests that spokesman represents." This gave First Amendment protection to unlimited spending by interests in initiative campaigns. The Court has struck down other attempts to limit the role of money in initiative politics. In 1988 it overturned a Colorado law banning paid petition circulators, and also voided a more recent Colorado law requiring paid petition circulators to wear name badges, be registered voters, and file detailed financial reports (Broder 2000, 67).

Contemporary initiative politics unleashes a vast wave of manipulative efforts at voters. Please sign this petition! Do not sign that petition! Please vote for this proposition! Vote against that proposition! Supporters of this proposition are skunks! That proposition will not work! Message clutter and confusion are inevitable, particularly in the states offering the most propositions in recent years: Oregon and California. Oregon is number one, offering ninety-seven initiatives between 1978 and 1998, an average of nine per election. In 1994–98, the average zoomed to fourteen. Nevertheless, even in states with fewer initiatives, or in states without initiatives, voters often confront statewide and local referenda in the polling booth, as I did in Northfield, Minnesota, on November 7, 2000. Knowing nothing about them, I refused to vote. My experience raises a worthwhile question—are voters competent to handle the heavy information demands initiative politics places upon them?

### Assessing Initiative Politics

The competence of initiative voters recently gained the increased attention of political scientists, and the results of their studies are mixed. Initiative elections place great burdens on voters, and many do the best they can. David Magleby's (1984) study found that voters did not heavily consult the initiative pamphlet circulated to all voters. In one initiative, a 1980 measure regarding rent control, "over three-fourths of the California voters did not match up their views on rent control with their votes on the measure" (144). Arthur Lupia (1994), studying voters' decisions on several California initiatives concerning the insurance industry in 1988, however, found more rational voter behavior. Those voters who merely knew the insurance industry's positions on the propositions made decisions similar to those made by voters who had high levels of factual knowledge about the propositions. Voters can take cues from who supports and opposes propositions, just as some follow cues from party labels. This sort of simplification is particularly useful for complex issues (like broad environmental initiatives) or narrow and uninteresting issues (such as the administration of state courts).

Will following cues always produce a vote in line with one's preferences under conditions of complete information? Political scientists are far from certain about this. Voters often reason based on feelings and dislikes rather than on relevant facts when following cues and shortcuts (Sniderman, Brody, and Tetlock 1991). Many voters may well follow their guts in voting, because they do not know the facts. Researchers found that initiative outcomes resembled the collective judgment of informed voters more closely when both sides contesting the issue spend heavily (Gerber and Lupia 1996). The more money spent, the more information available, and probably the more reliably people can follow cues to make choices consistent with their preferences. All this suggests that some voters may handle the challenge of initiatives well.

However, most do not, for three reasons. First, "lopsided spending in initiative politics is a regular occurrence, even more so than in candidate elections" (Ernst 2001, 1). With one side manipulating the arguments disproportionately, a rational vote becomes difficult. Second, even if voters correctly match ballot options and personal preferences, they do so on the basis of a quick and selfish calculation of what is best for them. Deliberation over the choice in a way that "refines and enlarges" one's perspective over the options is often totally absent here. Third, quick thinking on ballot propositions will omit careful contemplation of broader consequences. As Elizabeth Gerber (1999) puts it: "voters may not be able to anticipate the longer-run implications of their choices even if they are competent to figure out which policy alternative is more consistent with their preferences *at face value*" (145, emphasis added). The broader lesson is a simple one. The more knowledge an electoral system demands of voters, the harder rational voting becomes, and initiative systems dramatically raise the requisite levels of knowledge.

Given the limitations placed on voter competence by the initiative process, who reaps the greatest advantage from its politics? It is clear that organized interests are the big winners. They can put their cherished issue proposals before the public in undiluted forms. Some interests prosper more in initiative politics than do others, however. The most thorough research on the matter comes from the biggest initiative state, California. A recent study found that in California, "narrow based, well organized groups who seek to protect clearly identifiable interests and seek exclusive, divisible benefits for members" (such as corporations or unions) won passage of only 14 percent of the initiatives they proposed from 1986 to 1996 (Donovan et al. 1998, 82). Broader or more diffuse groups, representing environmentalists, homeowners, or consumers, often have fewer resources than corporations or unions. When confronting a narrow interest, however, broader groups prevailed on initiatives 35 percent of the time. When broad interests competed against each other over ballot issues in California, the sponsoring coalition won 58 percent of the time (95).

Even when a narrow interest loses, though, its proposal can move up the state political agenda. For example, unions placed initiatives 214 and 216 on the California ballot in 1996. Similar in content, the two initiatives sought to regulate state health maintenance organizations (HMOs). Although both failed, in the three months after the election, the legislature passed twenty-seven HMO regulation bills that included many provisions contained in the initiatives (Gerber 1999, 203). Narrow interests also excel at blocking initiatives sponsored by interests that are more diffuse. The 1986–96 California study revealed that narrow interests defeated other narrow interests 86 percent of the time and broader interests 65 percent of the time (Donovan et al. 1998, 95).

The evidence in support of broader and more diffuse interests prevailing in California may seem reassuring, but it easily overstates the democratic nature of initiative politics. First, is a "broad" interest necessarily superior to a "narrow" interest? It is true that narrow interests have strong economic incentives behind their actions, but corporations represent thousands of employees and shareholders. Unions represent thousands of workers. Their incentive structure may be narrow, but they do not necessarily represent a smaller slice of the public than do environmentalists, antigay rights organizations, government reform groups like Common Cause, or taxpayers' organizations. Such groups are parts of an activist stratum with far more knowledge than the vast majority of voters or citizens. In other words, regardless of the incentives behind group behavior, initiative politics today is not a vehicle for the direct voice of the people so much as a venue for elites to pursue their own agendas by manipulating popular preferences. The Populist vision underlying the reform is far from the present reality.

This point is underscored by the big role money plays in the process. It is true that money does not always determine initiative outcomes. Elizabeth Gerber's (1999) California research rejects "the allegation that economic groups buy policy outcomes through the direct legislation process.... The measures that economic groups support pass at a lower rate than those supported by citizens groups.... Even though economic interest groups spend a lot of money in the direct legislation process, this does not serve as proof that they now dominate the process" (137–40). Money does not always produce initiative *success* for big spenders. However, it does determine *agenda access* and thus structures the entire *pattern of manipulation* that characterizes initiative campaigns. Examples of narrow economic interests dominating the agenda are not hard to find in initiative politics. A narrow interest can win if it manipulates the dimensions of its issue the right way. In 1984, Californians approved an initiative creating a state lottery. The main sponsor of the initiative, Scientific Games corporation of Atlanta, artfully manipulated the dimensions of the issue. Advertisements claimed the lottery would pay for new school buildings and provide resources for deserving students. The lottery in fact gives school less than 3 percent of its revenue, but the public widely believes to this day that it is a major revenue source. Scientific Games, meanwhile, has reaped vast profits from its conduct of the lottery (Schrag 1998, 198).

Another pointed instance of money ruling the initiative process involved the case of Americans for Medical Rights in 1998. This interest group, formed by a mere three wealthy individuals, including the New York billionaire financier George Soros, sought to change the laws of five states. They advocated legalization of the possession and use of marijuana for people with a doctor's prescription. The group financed a successful 1996 California initiative and then paid to place similar measures before voters in Alaska, Colorado, Nevada, Oregon, and Washington. They heavily outspent their opposition in each state, which included federal drug czar Barry McCaffrey, who aggressively criticized the proposals. The wealthy three had their consultants flood the airwaves with advertisements presenting favorable dimensions of the initiative. Commercials usually featured a personal story of someone who could tell a compelling story of the humane benefits of medical marijuana. All five states passed the initiative, prompting one Arizona legislator to ask, "Why should a New York billionaire be writing the laws in Arizona?" (Broder 2000, 190–96).

The initiative process, then, is an agenda control game for unelected political elites who seek to manipulate the public into doing their bidding. Their success is variable, but the game has a high admission cost. Another "interest bias" exists in the composition of the electorate making the choices. Initiative voters are older, wealthier, and whiter than their states' populations, reflecting the bias that results from America's distinctively low-turnout elections (Cronin 1989, 74–77). Initiative campaigns follow the strategy of targeted activation, with messages closely fixed on likely voters who have little information or are undecided on the issue. The campaigns thus focus on a fraction of that half of the public that votes. The advertisements speak to their concerns, manipulating the dimensions of initiative issues toward the end of victory. It is an expensive variant of exclusive, interest-dominated politics. One can at least hope that the outcomes accurately reflect the actual preferences of the voters. However, we cannot expect this to happen with any acceptable level of reliability. The next section explains why.

### Nonexistent Mandates

A return to the social choice theory introduced in chapter 1 reveals how initiatives fail to reflect voters' preferences on policy issues. We have already noted that some political scientists find voters can act rationally in some initiative votes by pursuing simplifying cues (Lupia 1994; Donovan, Bowler, and McCuan 2001). Nevertheless, even if voters valiantly pursue rationality in the confusing muddle of initiative politics, the process is stacked against them. Agenda control by initiative formulators, manipulation of issue dimensions concerning each initiative, and strategic voting by citizens on initiatives make it impossible to discern a "will of the people" from direct votes on policy.

Political manipulation takes several forms in initiative politics. First, political activists push an issue before the public, manipulating the agenda for elite purposes. Second, advertising by proponents and opponents of each initiative is one long exercise in manipulation. Voters are presented with limited dimensions of complex issues in this ad war, often producing distorted understandings of what is at stake in an initiative. Manipulated understandings create false preferences, not a sincere public mandate. Finally, voters may vote strategically on initiatives, not pursuing their first choice but their strategic favorite among the manipulated choices placed before them.

However, even if voters have carefully reasoned, rational preferences on each of the options, voting in an initiative or a referendum cannot reliably reflect those preferences in the result. John Haskell (2001) developed two hypothetical examples from initiative politics that reveal this problem (142–44). Imagine a situation in which voters in a state face three pro-environment ballot propositions at the same time—Propositions A, B, and C. Any proposition garnering more than half of the votes becomes law. Proposition B is the most extreme, placing stringent new standards on state businesses. Propositions A and C place less-extensive regulations on companies in the state.

For simplicity's sake, imagine an electorate composed of three voters—Xenia, Yale, and Zed. And let's assume that, unlike in most elections, the voters are studious and will make careful judgments about each of the propositions before them. Moderates Xenia and Zed like both A and C but find Proposition B extreme. Yale, a strong environmentalist, strongly supports B but will also vote for A and C. After studying the issues, Xenia decides she will vote only for A. Zed, after similar study, opts only for C. The votes are cast as follows:

TABLE 4.2 Voter Preferences and Vote Results Concerning
Three Substantively Similar Initiatives

| Proposition | A | B | C |
|---|---|---|---|
| Xenia | Y | N | N |
| Yale | Y | Y | Y |
| Zed | N | N | Y |

Source: John Haskell, Direct Democracy or Representatitve Government? Dispelling the Populist Myth (Boulder, Colo.: Westview, 2001), 142.

Note that the winning combination, YNY, gained the support of none of the voters. Further, the majority of voters, consisting of Xenia and Zed, did not want both A and C to win, but both measures are now law. Why did this happen? As Haskell (2001) puts it: "the referendum process did not permit the voters to coalesce around what a majority of the voters thought was a coherent policy position [because] they had no mechanism to work out their differences" (142–43). The initiative process provides no opportunity for deliberation and compromise over such differences, and produces results that do not reflect, in this case, majority preferences.

Consider next a case in which two initiatives on criminal sentencing make the ballot. Proposition A imposes a mandatory life term on convicted possessors of a certain substantial amount of crack cocaine. Proposition B, listed below Proposition A on the ballot, requires a mandatory life term for possession of a certain amount of ordinary cocaine. Below are listed the preferences for voters Monica, Natalie, and Oscar, with NN indicating a preference for both measures failing and YY both passing, and so forth.

TABLE 4.3  Voter Preferences and Vote Results Concerning
Two Substantively Similar Initiatives

| Voters | First Choice | Second Choice | Third Choice | Fourth Choice |
|--------|--------------|---------------|--------------|---------------|
| Monica | YY | NN | YN | NY |
| Natalie | NN | YY | NY | YN |
| Oscar | YN | YY | NY | NN |

*Source*: John Haskell, *Direct Democracy or Representatitve Government? Dispelling the Populist Myth* (Boulder, Colo.: Westview, 2001), 143.

Monica's and Natalie's preferences differ dramatically, but both see the two propositions as linked. Both believe that each type of cocaine possession deserves similar punishment, though Natalie prefers neither and Monica both types of punishment. Monica views drug possession as strongly related to other crimes, whereas Natalie finds life in prison to be too harsh a sentence in either circumstance.

When the vote is taken, the crack referendum passes 2–1 with support from Monica and Oscar. Only Monica votes for the cocaine proposition, though, so it fails. However, if Natalie had known that the crack measure would pass, she would have changed her vote on the cocaine measure in the interest of fairness. Note that YY was her second choice and YN her fourth and last choice. But because of the *method* of voting, with each proposition considered separately (as they are in all states), it was impossible for Natalie to accurately reflect her preferences in this situation. The actual result, with one tough measure passing while the other fails, was strongly opposed by a majority of voters—in this case, Monica and Natalie.

As Haskell (2001) notes, the paradox of multiple elections on similar issues at the same time, as often happens in initiative states through counter-initiatives, "may well render the corporate judgment unsatisfactory to a majority a significant portion of the time" (144). His conclusion is a disturbing one:

> Voter rationality is in many ways *irrelevant* to the quality of the outcome of a plebiscite. *The outcome of a vote may be irrational, even when all of the participants are rational and informed.* And when the voters do have a preferred choice, it is not necessarily the case at all that the decision will reflect that.... The potential for manipulation always casts doubt on the validity of the final decision (144–45).

Haskell's conclusion applies to party-based elections as well as initiatives, meaning that "electoral arrangements ... are intrinsically flawed and can never be relied upon to identify the will of the people" (145). Ultimately, the debate over citizen competence is beside the point. Electoral procedures are chronically subject to manipulation, but, as Riker (1982) notes, we never know when manipulation produces the election result and when it genuinely represents popular preferences.

Is an election outcome the will of the people? Or is it the result of agenda control and the manipulation of issue dimensions by elites? Or the result of strategic voting by citizens that fails to represent their actual preferences? Or the result of election procedures, like those explained above, that distort popular preferences? The answers to such questions should guard us from expecting too much from elections.

Relying on elections to produce a coherent "will of the people" is an exercise in futility. Elections may represent that will; they may not. It is impossible to tell when they do. Election results are—unpredictably—the result of electoral rules and manipulations by political elites. Initiatives and referendums remain popular, however, because the public believes they are reliable mechanisms to impose their will and want them available for use (Hibbing and Theiss-Morse 1995, chapter 1). The public seldom lives up to their side of the bargain by following government and politics closely, though. And their reliable tool of elections is not reliable at all.

## In Defense of Legislative Decision Making

If initiatives are deeply flawed as a policymaking method, is the legislative process any better? The public does not think so. Many citizens view the give-and-take of lawmaking—involving public arguments over policy and eventual compromise—as highly distasteful. Legislators seem to many a group of backslapping, corrupt wheeler-dealers in the thrall of special interest groups. Such interests seek their own benefits at the expense of the broader public (Hibbing and Theiss-Morse 1995, chapter 1).

At times, this view may be accurate, but years of scholarly research present a different picture of legislatures. Political scientists widely agree that lawmakers are primarily motivated by their policy convictions, not corrupt personal gain (Fenno 1973, 1–2; Rosenthal 1998, 157–61). Our national and state legislatures are primarily organized around policy substance. Committee systems, in which policy ideas receive thorough consideration and deliberation, operate in all American legislatures. Lawmakers also derive much of their influence over legislation by demonstrating a command of policy substance when bills are considered in committee or on the chamber floor (Kingdon 1989, chapter 3).

Powerful interests can dominate legislative politics, but they also can so prevail in the initiative process. Campaign finance and lobbying regulation laws nationally and in many states have sharply eroded opportunities for shady and secretive group influence in legislatures. Interest groups are just one of several influences of legislative decision making, along with the views of constituents, the media, the executive branch and president or governor, lawmaking colleagues, legislative staff, and the lawmakers themselves (Kingdon 1989; Rosenthal 1998). Given the often slow pace and extensive deliberation evident in legislatures, it is usually the case that "very few represented groups are left out" when major legislation gradually moves toward enactment in law (Haskell 2001, 159). That does not mean that all interests get equal or fair representation in legislatures. Neither do they in initiative politics.

The legislative process possesses two primary advantages over initiatives as a means of making public policy. First, unlike initiatives, legislative lawmaking usually guarantees deliberation over major policy options. The initiative process produces decisions by merely requiring public voting. In contrast, legislative lawmaking mandates that those making the decisions "function in an institutional setting that fosters collective reasoning about common concerns" before votes are cast (Bessette 1994, 2). Deliberation is not always pretty, and a legislature, like the initiative process, is a venue for agenda manipulation and strategic voting. What results may not always be the highest sort of thinking about public ends, but it does have its virtues: "The deliberative process in the legislature may not be highly rational nor primarily analytical. But it does allow for different sides to make their case, opposing voices to be heard, and a settlement to be achieved" (Rosenthal 1998, 161). And unlike the initiative process, legislative lawmaking provides ample opportunities to correct past mistakes: "For all of their failings, legislatures have the singular virtue of being capable of identifying, correcting and learning from past errors" (Ellis 2002, 201). Further, legislative deliberation gets frequent and thorough media coverage, giving the public many opportunities to inspect the proceedings.

A second vital advantage that legislative lawmaking possesses over initiative politics lies with the superior accountability available for legislative actions. Lawmakers' votes are public knowledge and help voters to reward or punish incumbents at election time. Lawmakers are up for regular reelection, but successful initiatives remain law forever unless a costly and lengthy repeal process ultimately succeeds, which it rarely does. Recent complaints that legislators "run scared" and provide "responsiveness without responsibility" reveal that the accountability function is alive and well (Anthony King 1997, 3; Jacobson 1997, 208). Party-based accountability is preferable to the individualistic accountability for lawmakers prevalent in America, but the ability to hold government accountable is much more readily available to the public in legislative politics than in initiative politics.

## THE UTILITY OF ELECTIONS

Elections thus remain useful primarily as mechanisms for enforcing accountability upon elected officials. Any incumbent remains at risk of losing her/his job due to the wrath of the voters. Without that essential check, basic liberties would vanish.

That check also helps to inform legislative deliberations with a concern with public sentiment. These are all vital functions of elections, but that is the extent of them. We cannot rely on elections to translate a coherent popular mandate for a policy or party into office. Political elites effectively distort the dimensions of ballot issues and manipulate the substantive choice through agenda control. And doing this, having an impact on such election outcomes, costs big money. The price of admission for influence is high. Even if voters have reliable knowledge and clear preferences when they vote, which happens far less often than it should, electoral rules cannot reliably translate these preferences into results. Ultimately, exercises in direct democracy are exercises in futility.

One partial exception to the above problems lies in recall elections. They usually feature high turnout and a simple binary choice to keep or eject an elected official—the very definition of an accountability election. The threat of a recall, however, can impede legislative deliberation. Referenda require too much of voters, empower political elites, and cannot necessarily produce reliable policy verdicts. At least referenda result from the deliberative processes of the state legislature. The initiative remains the least defensible direct democracy reform of all. It bypasses legislative deliberation, permits direct agenda control by unelected political elites, facilitates influence by big spenders, creates a long ballot that exhausts voters, and produces election results that do not reliably reflect popular preferences. There is no defense for the initiative and its politics.

The American political system must change if it is to reliably provide high turnout, political stability, accountability for electoral officials, and deliberation in government. Finding our way to reforms that enhance turnout, accountability, stability, and deliberation requires that we understand the political battles waged currently over the electoral system. Most recent controversies about the electoral arrangements have addressed these four goals, but usually indirectly. Contemporary combat over the electoral system concerns matters that divide political elites—parties, interests, candidates, and officeholders—often on partisan grounds. It is to these tussles that we next turn.

CHAPTER 5

# Four Controversies

F our disputes over the electoral system have garnered extensive attention in recent years. The four sources of controversy are the electoral
college, state and local election administration, the decennial census
count and legislative redistricting procedures, and U.S. House districts
drawn according to the racial characteristics of state populations. None
of these issues are likely to rank anywhere near the top of a list of "most
important issues" identified by the American public. They are complex
matters that seldom get sustained media attention. Political elites, though,
have lavished considerable attention on each of these issues, for several
reasons. First, they often reflect partisan divisions. Republicans and Democrats differ on most of these issues, with each party making principled
arguments that coincide with its partisan interests. In addition, important
interest groups—such as the National Association for the Advancement
of Colored People (NAACP), Common Cause, and the AFL-CIO—have
pushed their own positions regarding these controversies. A small but significant group of political activists in the American population has devoted
time, oratory, and resources to the issues as well. Along with campaign
finance (addressed in chapter 6), the four matters listed above comprise
the top electoral reform topics of recent years.

All four matters affect important goals of the electoral system in note-
worthy ways. The debate over whether to reform or replace the electoral
college involves defining how the electoral system should allow the public
to hold a president accountable for actions in office. Revising the administration of elections affects their operation as a means of accountability and
may strongly influence electoral turnout. Census counting and redistricting

help to determine the arrangement of national and state legislative representation, also crucially shaping the accountability function of the electoral system. Drawing districts according to racial population patterns sparks a debate about differing definitions of legislative accountability, one that emphasizes the importance of racial difference and another that centers on the "color blind" equality of all citizens. The structure of racial representation also influences substantive deliberation in governmental councils. Controversies around these issues can alter American political, governmental, and even regime stability. These are matters of consequence.

## The Debate over the Electoral College

The fact that a popular-vote loser can triumph in the electoral college and become president is controversial in both democratic theory and practical politics. The electoral college awarded George W. Bush the presidency in 2000 despite his receiving one-half million fewer popular votes than Al Gore. Polls at the time showed a majority of Americans wished to replace the electoral college with a system of direct popular election (*ABC News/Washington Post* Poll 2000), but a substantial majority of the public also indicated they accepted George W. Bush as the legitimate winner of the presidency (*Newsweek* Poll 2000; Gallup Poll 2000). The public accepted the legitimacy of these Constitutional arrangements, but also wanted them changed for the future. Some national legislators, including the recently elected Senator Hillary Clinton of New York, urged a constitutional amendment for direct popular election. As months passed, however, the issue faded from the national agenda, receiving little media or governmental attention one year after the election.

The modern electoral college is the product of another electoral crisis that spawned the Twelfth Amendment to the Constitution. The original language of Article II provided for an electoral college, composed of members elected by state legislatures after a popular election. Each state's delegation equaled its combined number of U.S. Representatives and Senators. The candidate receiving the most votes from the electoral college would become president; the candidate with the second highest total would become vice president. In 1800, Thomas Jefferson and his running mate, Aaron Burr, received an equal number of electoral votes. Burr then aggressively sought the presidency, and the election went to the House for resolution. Only after several ballots and political machinations by Alexander Hamilton did Jefferson win the House vote. Burr repaid Hamilton for their long-standing rivalry by killing him in a duel in 1804. That same year, a proposed solution gained ratification as a constitutional amendment. The Twelfth Amendment provided for separate electoral college votes for president and vice president. Should no candidate receive a majority of electoral college votes, the top three finishers would vie in the House for the presidency, with each state delegation casting one vote. The Senate would choose between the top two vice presidential finishers.

The Constitution makes elections an exercise in federalism. Each state conducts a separate presidential election, with its legislature deciding how to allocate electoral college votes. Since the mid-nineteenth century, states have allocated their electoral college votes in a plurality winner-take-all fashion, in order to maximize their impact on the aggregate outcome. The two current exceptions to this pattern are Maine and Nebraska, each of which allocates votes to U.S. House district plurality winners, with two votes to the statewide popular vote plurality winner.

Bush's 2000 victory was not the first by a loser of the popular vote. None of the prior outcomes, though, triggered a serious consideration of constitutional change. After the crisis that spawned the Twelfth Amendment, the electoral college has failed to elect the popular-vote winner four (arguably, five) times. In 1824, John Quincy Adams finished well behind Andrew Jackson in both the popular and electoral college vote (31.9 percent and 84 votes versus 42.2 percent and 99 votes), but won the presidency anyway. After much negotiation and many ballots, Adams won in the House, though he eventually lost both the popular and electoral college votes to Jackson in 1828.

Rutherford B. Hayes defeated Samuel Tilden 185 to 184 in the 1876 electoral college vote, despite finishing approximately 500,000 votes behind Tilden in the popular vote. The period after the popular vote involved much partisan squabbling about the electoral votes of three southern states—South Carolina, Florida, and Louisiana. Congress appointed an election commission that awarded the disputed electoral college votes to Hayes. The Republican vote-grab seems blatant, and was accomplished only by preventing a vote overturning the result by the Democrat-controlled Congress. Republicans forestalled this by agreeing to the withdrawal of federal troops from the South, ending reconstruction. The three disputed states also featured much election fraud that prevented African Americans from voting (Hardaway 1994, 130–33), making it hard to label the Democrats as innocent victims. As in 2000, partisan knives came out on both sides during a disputed presidential election.

The 1888 election resulted in Grover Cleveland's loss of his White House incumbency to Benjamin Harrison. Harrison won a substantial electoral college majority (233 to 168) despite receiving about 95,000 fewer popular votes than did Cleveland. Harrison won a number of large northeastern and midwestern states by modest margins, whereas Cleveland rolled up large majorities in the Democratic "solid South." The election featured much less controversy over vote fraud and disputed electoral votes, and the result was accepted calmly by the public.

The most controversial recent election before 2000 occurred in 1960, won by John F. Kennedy by 303 to 219 in the electoral college. To this day, it is not entirely clear whether John F. Kennedy or Richard M. Nixon won a plurality of the popular vote in that election. Charges of vote fraud were rampant in Illinois, which went to Kennedy by a slim margin of 8,858 votes out of 4,757,409 cast. A joke at the time had Bobby Kennedy calling Democratic Mayor Richard J. Daley of Chicago and asking him now many votes JFK could expect from the city. Daley's reply: "How many do you need?" Had Kennedy lost Illinois and Texas (which he carried by 46,233 votes), he would have lost in the electoral college.

The major problem in determining the 1960 popular vote winner lies with the Alabama results. On the Alabama ballot that year were Republican electors pledged to Nixon, national Democratic electors pledged to Kennedy, and a set of "states rights" conservative Democratic electors pledged to Senator Harry Byrd of Virginia. Though the Byrd slate won six of the eleven electoral votes from the state, Kennedy is often awarded the entire Democratic popular vote in Alabama, resulting in a national Kennedy plurality of 112,000 votes. If one divides the Alabama Democratic votes proportionately between the Kennedy and Byrd slates, Nixon ekes out a 50,000 vote popular plurality (Longley and Pierce 1999, 50). When he met with Kennedy to discuss the result shortly after Election Day, Kennedy allegedly greeted him with: "Well, Dick, we'll never know who won that election, will we?" Nixon considered challenging the popular vote results in several states but relented in the interest of regime stability. Because most observers credited Kennedy with a popular and electoral college victory, controversy over the election soon subsided.

The remarkable result of the 2000 election also produced a rather limited outcry, despite Bush's election after losing the popular vote and the unsettling turmoil over the awarding of Florida's electoral votes that persisted until the Supreme Court decision of *Bush v. Gore* in mid-December.

Though critics of the electoral college had predicted that such an outcome would spawn a legitimacy crisis for American government (Longley and Pierce 1999), none materialized.

## THE FOUNDERS' LOGIC AND ITS DEFENSE

Given many Americans' grudging acceptance of George W. Bush as their legitimate president in 2000, criticisms of the electoral college abound. Many find it hard to square the operation of the institution with the basic principles of democratic theory that prescribe equal voting power for all citizens. Under the electoral college, some citizens' votes are more consequential than are others. Lawrence Longley and Neil Pierce (1999) calculate that certain voters hold disproportionate influence. They include voters in very small states, due to their overrepresentation in the Senate, and those in the very largest states (Illinois, Texas, Florida, Pennsylvania, New York, and California) because of their huge contribution to the vote totals (152–53). Longley and Pierce also find that the institution gives an advantage to Latino/a, urban, and Jewish voters because of their concentration in the largest states, but not African-American voters (153–54). Some African-American leaders have defended the electoral college, though, because it gives great influence to large states with high African-American populations (*Congressional Quarterly* 1979, 78).

Given that the electoral college creates unequal voting power in the electorate, by what logic was it formed in the first place? At the Constitutional Convention (convened in 1787), James Madison and several other large-state delegates favored direct popular election of the president. The differing suffrage requirements of the states constituted a big obstacle to this goal. Southern states prevented slaves from voting, and several states retained property requirements for the franchise. By using the electoral college, the founders could avoid battles over the vexing differences in voting rights across states.

The institution was a compromise between the small state forces at the convention that preferred equal state influence in presidential selection and large states wanting a direct popular vote. After lengthy negotiations, a deal was struck. It allowed state power to operate in choosing presidents based on congressional apportionment. Both equal state representation in the Senate and apportionment by population in the House figured in the electoral college outcome. One provision that reassured small states moved the election to the House with each state delegation casting one vote should the electoral college not produce a majority winner. The compromise won acceptance because of the widespread belief that George Washington, the consensus choice, would serve as the first president. In addition, delegates believed that "once Washington had finished his tenure as president, the electors would cease to provide majorities and the chief executive would usually be chosen by the House" (Roche 1961, 811). James Madison later described the electoral college as "the result of compromise between the larger and smaller states, giving to the latter the advantage of selecting a president from the candidates, in consideration of the former in selecting the candidates from the people" (Pierce and Longley 1981, 17).

Defenders of the electoral college hold that it is democratic in spirit and operation, but that its democratic operation is tempered by a federal structure. Martin Diamond argues that:

> In fact, presidential elections are already just about as democratic as they can be. We already have one-man, one-vote, *but in the states.* Elections are as freely and democratically contested as elections can be—but *in the states.* Victory always goes democratically to the winner of the raw popular vote— *but in the states....* Whatever we decide, then, democracy itself is not at stake in our decisions, only the prudential question of how to channel and organize the popular will.... There is no reason, then, why the president, admittedly the representative of all of us, cannot represent us and hence be elected by us in a way corresponding to our compoundly federal and national character" (Diamond 1977, 7–8).

Diamond also contends that complaints about the electoral college reflect a disapproval of the district system of election. "The possibility cannot be removed that the winner of a majority of the districts may also not be the winner of the raw popular vote" (Diamond 1977, 9). This happened in Great Britain in 1974, when the Labour party won three more seats than the Conservatives and formed the next government, though it re- ceived fewer popular votes than the Conservatives. District elections and the electoral college, Diamond notes, "allow local democratic responsive- ness to geographically based minorities whose interests otherwise might be utterly neglected" because in the electoral college "power will be nationally distributed, rather than concentrated in regional majorities" (Diamond 1977, 10–11). The key to this argument is Diamond's definition of state- level elections for president as fundamentally democratic. Are they?

## CRIES FOR REFORM

Critics of the electoral college deploy an array of arguments against it. Every other democracy in the world that elects a chief executive does it through direct popular vote, adopting a national, not federal, definition of "one-person, one-vote." The majority of Americans who favor direct popular election of the president also opt for this national definition of voting power. Lawrence Longley and Neil Pierce (1999) present five major criticisms of the institution. First, the electoral college is a "distorted counting device" of the popular will because its votes are allocated for ten years based on an increasingly outdated census, and it also overrepresents small states due to their Senate seats. Second, candidate electoral strategies are derived from these distortions and focus on large states that are electorally competitive, ignoring most of the other states. Third, the parochial needs of closely fought large states get disproportionate emphasis in national government and policy thanks to the electoral college. Fourth, the electoral college greatly favors the two major party candidates who have the best chances at statewide pluralities and helps only those minor party candidates with a strong regional following in a few states. Fifth, no effective method exists to require electors to vote for the candidate they have pledged to support. Though fifteen states have laws requiring electors to vote as pledged, the laws can only operate after the rogue vote is cast and the damage is done. Wayward electors have cast rogue votes eight times in American history. In a close election, such flukes could be determinative (160–67). If George W. Bush had lost three electoral votes to Al Gore, Gore would have won the presidency. As it was, one rogue elector defected from Al Gore, yielding him 266 electoral votes instead of the 267 to which he was entitled.

A summary phrase for these problems comes from John Anderson (2000), an independent candidate for president in 1980: the electoral college "undercuts accountability" to the national electorate (1). However, as noted earlier, the principle of accountability is a debatable one here. The electoral college does provide federal accountability, and its winner-take-all provisions usually magnify the popular vote winner's margin of victory, also facilitating regime stability. The principle of federal accountability is structured permanently into the constitution. The founders provided for federal accountability in the Senate, as in the electoral college, and explicitly forbade any alteration of Senate apportionment.

The electoral college does not seem to greatly influence overall election turnout. The institution's main effect is to structure the strategic targeting of presidential campaigns in particular ways. It is not obvious that abolishing it will make presidential campaign appeals any less exclusive than they already are. The institution also promotes political stability by favoring the two-party system. Without the electoral college and SMP district elections, the electoral arena would be crowded with multiple parties and increasing clutter, perhaps making accountability more difficult and governmental stability less certain.

The arguments on the issue's other side are equally forceful. National accountability is the common basis for electing chief executives among the world's democracies. Voting equality among citizens may seem essential in selecting a president, the most important office in the nation. It is far from obvious that reforming the electoral college will destabilize governments or the political system. It may improve accountability by promoting a less exclusive focus on large, competitive states in election campaigns. The growth of minor parties also can boost the accountability of government for perspectives heretofore marginalized by the electoral system. And the problem of faithless electors cries out for an immediate solution.

## THE REFORM ALTERNATIVES

Three major alternatives receive advocacy by proponents of electoral college reform. The most frequently mentioned alternative would abolish the electoral college and provide for a direct election in which the leading candidate wins the presidency if she/he receives at least 40 percent of the popular vote. If no candidate reaches that threshold, a runoff featuring the top two finishers would ensue. Every vote would count equally in either outcome, and the winner would always have the most popular votes. The plan would also encourage minor parties and perhaps invest them with considerable influence in the outcome should a runoff become necessary. This would broaden accountability to viewpoints previously ignored by the political system (Whitaker 2001, 16).

Opponents of the reform argue that giving minor parties an advantage would threaten political stability. Presidential elections could resemble the arcane maneuverings involved in creating coalition governments in proportional representation election systems. It would be unlikely that candidates would exceed the 40 percent threshold as minor parties arose, and the negotiation and coalition building between the first and second rounds would confuse citizens and give disproportionate influence to extreme views represented by the minor parties. Defenders of American federalism also oppose the system for its abolition of federal accountability as represented in the electoral college.

A more modest reform involves apportioning individual electoral votes on the basis of plurality results in House districts, with each state also allocating their two "Senate" electoral votes to the statewide plurality winner. As mentioned previously, Maine and Nebraska already allocate their electoral votes this way at present. Proponents of the "district plan" argue that it will produce results closer to the popular vote than does the current winner-take-all method. It also preserves the present electoral college allocation of votes that gives small states an advantage. The plan also better represents the diversity of opinion within states and encourages presidential candidates to campaign with House candidates of the same party. This might strengthen the role of parties in elections and make coordinated control of the presidency and Congress more likely (Durbin 2001, 27; Schier 2000, 218–19). The plan could bring a new party-based accountability to presidential and congressional elections, while preserving a disaggregated form of federal accountability in presidential contests.

There are several arguments in opposition to this plan. It remains possible to win the electoral vote while losing the popular vote under this method, bringing into question the plan's accountability to the wishes of voters. Under this plan, Nixon would have defeated Kennedy in 1960, despite Kennedy's claim to have won the popular vote, and Jimmy Carter would have tied Gerald Ford in the 1976 election though he won the popular vote (Dudley and Gitelson 2001, 150–51). The system still preserves a winner-take-all allocation of electoral votes, putting minor parties at a disadvantage. Some analysts, however, hold that by disaggregating statewide winner-take-all, minor parties are actually encouraged (Sayre and Parris 1970, 102–17). Proponents of national accountability in presidential elections find the district plan to be no solution at all.

A particularly elaborate reform is the "proportional plan," which introduces proportional representation into the electoral college. Most proportional plans divide statewide electoral votes into thousandths of votes (to the third decimal point). The election threshold could be set at a majority or perhaps 40 percent of electoral votes. Should all candidates fall below the election threshold percentage, the House and Senate in joint session would choose the winners between the two top vote-getting tickets. Proponents note that this aligns the electoral college result closely with the popular vote but retains the current allocation of electoral votes among states. Election results like those of 1876, 1888, and 2000 become unlikely under this plan. Presidential campaigns would focus less on large states and become more national in scope. It would also give minor parties a much better chance of winning electoral votes.

And that, according to opponents, is one of the plan's many problems. By dividing the votes proportionately, a conclusive result becomes less likely. Federal accountability to states also disappears under this plan because it eliminates the states' ability to set their own rules for allocating electoral votes. The 40-percent threshold also raises questions. Should not a candidate have to get at least 50 percent to avoid a congressional vote on the matter (Whitaker 2001, 20)? And if the proportional allocation roughly mirrors the popular vote, why not simply make the popular vote determinative?

One reform proposal is less controversial, and for that reason, is unlikely to be enacted. The "automatic plan" would abolish the office of elector and simply award votes automatically to candidates who win statewide pluralities. It is hard to think of any reason for keeping electors around, because states and candidates want the votes registered automatically. Automatic electoral college voting is entirely consistent with the present system and involves only minor change. Because "faithless electors" have yet to produce a flawed electoral college result, though, the reform targets an issue that receives little attention in the debate over the electoral college. Many reformers think it involves inadequate tinkering with the status quo, whereas defenders of the current system fail to see an urgent need for such reform. Thus, the most broadly defensible reform of all lies unused.

How do these proposed changes compare with the present system in their effects upon the stability, turnout, accountability, and deliberation provided by the electoral system? The current system, as well as all of the reforms, claim to enhance accountability, they just differ in the type of accountability that they provide. The current system and the automatic plan rest clearly on the principle of federal accountability, with presidential elections organized as a series of concurrent but separate state elections. The district and proportional plans keep one aspect of federal accountability——the allocation of electoral votes to states—but include heavy doses of other accountability principles as well. The district plan organizes the results on a more popular than federal basis, by allocating results according to House district results. So, likewise, does the proportional plan, with statewide PR as its basis. Both lie somewhere between federal and national accountability, making them two different versions of mixed accountability systems, one statewide and proportional and another statewide and district winner-take-all. Direct popular election, in contrast, rests squarely on a principle of equal national accountability to all voters in the nation, whose votes all count equally in determining the outcome.

It is difficult to assess the impact of the various plans on presidential election turnout. The proportional and direct popular election plans could stimulate higher turnout if citizens perceive that their votes count more directly in the selection of a president. The proportional and direct popular vote plans, however, promise less political and governmental stability because they encourage minor parties and thus may produce less conclusive election results. The automatic plan and the current electoral college format offer no change in political, governmental, or regime stability. Party-based accountability may arise from the district plan through its transformation of presidential elections into more party-based affairs. That may bring a strong party basis to national government, also strengthening governmental stability. Do any of the alternatives affect governmental deliberation? Any such effects would likely be small. The district plan might boost partisan deliberation a bit, and the proportional and direct election plans may require more coalition-building deliberation in a more complex electoral order.

The electoral college "problem" is not as simple as it might seem upon first inspection, and the reform alternatives have highly variable qualities. Debate over reform promises to persist for many years because the immediate probability of change is slight: "It is extremely unlikely that even a simple majority of states would ratify an amendment abolishing the electoral college, much less the 38 required constitutionally. Only a handful of senators have voiced support for the idea; and the Senate, holding great power, will be a long time coming around on the issue" (Raskin 2001, 11). More reflection about the consequences of change is needed in the future. As political scientist Nelson Polsby warns: "Before you make a big change in institutions, you should do some run-throughs and think about what would happen" (quoted in "Pondering the Fate" 2000, 1). Any "run-through" should consider the consequences for political stability and accountability, voter turnout, and the quality of deliberation in government.

## The Uproar over Election Administration

The simple act of casting a ballot is not so simple to arrange. The public expects balloting to be administered fairly. Voters must be properly identified, directed to the right polling place, and allowed to vote via reliable and comprehendible methods. After the polls close, the tabulations should be timely and accurate. The irregularities concerning the 2000 voting process in Florida and other states have eroded public confidence in the fairness of elections. In 1996, three-quarters of the population thought the election had been at least somewhat fair. After 2000, that proportion fell to about one-half (*National Election Study* 1996; 2000).

Though Florida's elections suffered from multiple irregularities, other states had problems conducting the balloting as well. Illinois, South Carolina, and Georgia all had higher rates of spoiled ballots than did Florida. In Chicago, almost one in ten presidential ballots did not register a vote (Caltech 2001, 7). The problems in Florida, of course, gained wide notoriety because of the unusually close presidential result there. The battle over Florida produced several serious criticisms of the American system of election administration. The U.S. Commission on Civil Rights produced a controversial report claiming the election was marked by "injustice, ineptitude and inefficiency" to the disadvantage of minorities (Farris 2001, 3). Republican members of the Commission disputed these findings and conclusions. Irregular procedures for counting overseas military ballots in Florida and other states led to cries that America's fighting men and women had been unfairly disenfranchised. The variation in ballot procedures and equipment from county to county in Florida and other states affected the reliability of the vote count. As discussed previously, disputed recount procedures in Florida led to historic rulings by the Florida and U.S. Supreme Courts. Part of that controversy involved the counting of "overvotes"—ballots on which two or more presidential votes were cast—and "undervotes"—ballots with no discernable presidential vote. The 2000 election's beehive of controversies underscores the previously unremarked importance of election administration in American politics.

## How We Register and Vote

An absence of close presidential elections in the twenty years before 2000 blinded most Americans to the remarkably elaborate operations involved in administering elections. "The last presidential election involved more than 100 million voters casting ballots at more than 190,000 polling places, staffed by more than 1.4 million regular or temporary administrators or poll workers" (National Commission on Federal Election Reform 2001, 25). Actual administration of this vast apparatus is primarily a county or a city government responsibility. Decisions on voting technologies lie at that level as well, producing voting methods that vary from county to county in Florida, as well as other states. The national average of county operating expenses to conduct elections in 2000 was about $10 per vote, with some rural counties spending far more than that (National Commission on Federal Election Reform 2001, 68).

The cost and responsibility fall on counties because of decisions made by state governments that are constitutionally charged with the administration of elections. Article 1, Section 4 of the U.S. Constitution states that "The Times, Places and Manner of Holding Elections for Senators and Representatives, shall be prescribed in each State by the legislature thereof; but Congress may at any time by Law make or alter such Regulations, except as to Places of choosing Senators." Alexander Hamilton, in *Federalist #59,* explained that the Constitution "reserved to the national authority a right to interpose, whenever extraordinary circumstance might render that interposition necessary to its safety." Hamilton argued that this residual national authority was necessary to prevent the national government from owing its existence "to the pleasure of state governments" (Hamilton [1788] 1961, 362–63).

The federal courts have long ruled that Congress has broad authority to regulate national legislative elections, holding that the state power to set neutral rules for the time, place, and manner of elections may be superceded by the national government.[1] A recent, dramatic example of this federal power is the National Voter Registration Act of 1993, upheld by the courts even though it told states precisely how to register voters for federal elections, right down to the registration form (National Commission on Federal Election Reform 2001, 22). Known as the "motor voter" act, the law requires states to allow voter registration at driver licensing bureaus and permits optional state voter registration programs at other governmental locations, such as welfare offices. Motor voter has boosted the number of Americans registered to vote, but has not increased election turnout.

Voter registration began in the late nineteenth century as a Progressive reform, adopted by states to curb vote fraud. Originally, counties and cities operated most registration systems. Voters commonly had to reregister every two to four years, and more often than that if they changed addresses. As noted in chapter 3, this demanding system helped to lower turnout in the early twentieth century. In the 1960s, court litigation and civil rights laws removed some of the more restrictive practices of local registration systems. Now, no state can close its registration rolls more than thirty days before an election, and more jurisdictions have adopted permanent registration, shedding the requirement for regular re-registration.

Another recent registration reform involves the adoption of a statewide registration system that creates one central record of registrants. This central file can be computerized and made instantly available to any county or city registration office or polling place on Election Day, greatly reducing impediments to voting. Eleven states and the District of Columbia have statewide systems, seven more have adopted them and three are in the process of creating them. Florida recently enacted the reform in response to the 2000 election troubles in that state.

At the center of election administration is the ballot itself. Until the late 1880s, parties used to print them themselves. Publicly printed secret paper ballots were the norm in America until the 1940s, when voting machines and punch-card ballots arrived. A newer electronic method began use in the 1980s, involving "optical scan" ballots in which a voter must connect a line or circle an item, much as a student does on a standardized test form. More recently, some counties and cities have adopted electronic "touch screen" voting. Voters press items on an electronic monitor to cast their ballot.

The reliability of these methods varies greatly. A postelection study by faculty at the California and Massachusetts Institutes of Technology presented comprehensive evidence on the performance of differing balloting methods. Paper ballots—whether optically scanned or hand-counted—proved the most reliable in the 2000 election. In the presidential race, only 1.8 percent of paper ballots and 1.5 percent of scanned ballots were "residual votes," meaning the vote's content could not be determined. Punch-card ballots have a 50 percent higher error rate, with voting machines performing significantly worse than any of the other systems. The practical consequences of differing balloting technologies are big. Over 30 million voters used punch ballots in 2000. Had they used optical scanning, 300,000 more presidential and 420,000 more Senate and gubernatorial votes would have been recorded reliably. Had voting machines not been in use, an estimated 830,000 more Senate and gubernatorial votes would have resulted (Caltech 2001, 21–22).

The presence of punch cards in Florida raised very difficult questions about what constitutes a valid vote. Arguments over the status of a "chad," the sections of ballots punched out to indicate a vote, raged for weeks in county election administration offices, the state legislature, state courts, and the national media. This tempest was very much the product of the punch-card technology. Disputed ballots are much less frequent with optical scan and paper ballot technologies. The Caltech MIT report (2001) recommends widespread adoption of optical scan technology because of its superior efficiency over traditional paper ballots and greater reliability than machines, electronic voting, or punch cards (3).

## THE CURRENT DISPUTES

Beyond ballot specifics, several major controversies arose from the administration of the 2000 election. One is the patchwork system of registration, which raises questions about accountability and turnout in America's electoral system. If variable registration laws prevent otherwise qualified citizens from voting, turnout falls and it becomes more difficult for the collective citizenry to hold government accountable. Flawed voting technologies also hinder direct lines of accountability between citizens and their government, as do unclear or disputed standards about what constitutes a valid vote. Problems and perceptions of unequal access to polling places may have reduced turnout in 2000. They also raise accountability concerns and, if allowed to persist, call into question the very legitimacy and stability of the electoral system itself. America's federal structure, however, complicates discussion of problems and solutions. Should the national government mandate and fund election administration standards in the states? If so, how extensively? Which state variations are desirable and which indefensible?

Over fifty election administration reform bills appeared in Congress by late 2001, emblematic of the renewed national agenda status of these controversies. Four national commissions produced recommendations varying in their assessment of the scope of the problems and in their prescriptions for an enhanced federal role: the aforementioned Caltech MIT Voting Technology Project, the Constitution Project, the National Commission on Federal Election Reform, and the National Task Force on Election Reform. The Bush administration endorsed the recommendations of the National Commission on Federal Election Reform, which advocated at most a very modest increase in the national government's role in election administration and called on states to enact most of the desired changes. Electoral reform was not near the top of the administration's agenda, and Congress, beset by equal partisan divisions, did not rapidly reach a consensus. Still, several points in the commission reports guided congressional rethinking of American election administration.

First, America's patchwork voter registration system had great consequences in the excruciatingly close 2000 election. The Census Bureau estimates that three million registered voters did not vote in 2000 because of registration problems. The Caltech MIT study argues that registration systems should be complete, accurate, free of fraud, and usable at polling places and should involve easy registration procedures (56–57). The most efficient way to achieve these standards is for states to computerize a statewide registration system, a reform recommended by the Caltech MIT Voting Technology Project, the National Commission on Federal Election Reform, and the Constitution Project's Forum on Election Reform. Another possible solution to this is provisional voting, in which a disputed registrant can complete a ballot at the polls that would be counted if the registration problem is subsequently resolved. A related but more difficult question concerns funding such systems. Should this be left up to the states or should the federal government fund all or part of it? Many other democracies operate national voter registration systems, and Congress could conceivably fund one. This goes very much against the grain of American federalism, however, and has no vocal advocates at present. But it is worth considering.

Second, though it is clear that some balloting technologies are more reliable than are others, adopting new technologies raises a host of questions. Who should pay for it? Who should decide the appropriate technology of particular cities, counties, and states? The National Task Force on Election Reform (2001) holds that the main problem is not so much particular technologies as it is "central count systems" in which punch cards, touch screen, or optical-scan ballots are counted in one total with no record of individual votes retained. In this system, voters cannot be notified of their errors at the polling place (24). Should national or state law ban certain systems and forms of ballots?

Third, several commissions are particularly critical of states that allow early voting at election offices before election day (as in Texas), internet voting (thus far only attempted in the 2000 Arizona Democratic presidential primary), mail ballots (used in Oregon), and liberal absentee balloting rules (half of all ballots cast in the state of Washington in 2000 were absentee). The Forum on Election Reform argues that these methods do not satisfy five essential objectives for election administration. They are: "(1) assure the privacy of the secret ballot and protection against coerced voting, (2) verify that only duly registered voters cast ballots, (3) safeguard ballots against loss of alternation, (4) assure their prompt counting, and

(5) foster the communal aspect of citizens voting together" (Forum on Election Reform 2001, 14). The director of elections for Washington State, however, takes strong exception to these criteria: "No consideration is given to the point of view that one reason western states have enhanced voting by mail is because THE VOTERS LIKE IT! It is convenient for them, and they appreciate the extra time it gives them to consider the various choices and make informed, intelligent decisions" (Forum on Election Reform 2001, 36–37). Voter convenience may help turnout, but perhaps at the expense of proper accountability, given increased possibilities for fraud and coercion with these alternative voting methods. Which criterion is superior in this case—turnout or accountability?

Fourth, several commissions recommend establishing clear and consistent rules for identifying what constitutes a vote and for the timetables and procedures for contesting an election result. Dispute over vagueness in Florida's recount law inflamed the controversy over the election result in 2000. The Supreme Court in *Bush v. Gore* held that voters in states should be given "equal protection of the law" in assuring that all votes are counted equally. However, determining the legitimacy of a vote is at times a difficult task. Overvotes, for two or more candidates, and undervotes, for no candidate, can have very different meanings. Though most overvotes are mistakes, about 70 percent of undervotes are not. An estimated one million presidential ballots in 2000 were deliberately unmarked (National Task Force 2001, 25). Developing clear standards for disputed votes is not easy, but certain technologies make overvoting less common and are at least a partial solution to the problem. The National Commission on Federal Election Reform (2001) recommends Florida's 2001 law regarding election disputes. The law clearly separates the contest phase, involving litigation and taking of evidence, from the actual vote count and certification process that precedes it (62). Are uniform national definitions of a vote and regulations regarding contesting an election result necessary?

Fifth, concern about equal access to the polling place is an incendiary issue with the potential to damage American race relations. The U.S. Commission on Civil Rights did document several instances of inadequate election administration in America in racial minority neighborhoods, but the Commission's claim of conscious attempts to intimidate minority voters has drawn criticism. Either problem, if proven true, damages the turnout and accountability of the electoral system. The problem of unequal election administration, however, is complicated by evidence from a study by political scientists Martha Kropf and Steven Knack. They found that African Americans live disproportionately in counties with more reliable ballot technologies. Antiquated equipment is preponderantly located in counties with large white and Republican majorities. Latino/as are most likely to vote with punch-card systems, particularly because of their heavy population in Los Angeles County, where punch cards are employed. California uses punch cards extensively because they easily accommodate the complex state ballot with its many referenda (reported in Pruden 2001). (However, in mid-2001, the California Secretary of State decertified two types of punch-card technologies that produce chad, but retained certification of the Datavote system, which does not [Seelye 2001].) The question of race and ballot technology is thus a complex one that is not amenable to a sweeping solution. How can we ensure proper accountability and turnout without racial discrimination? A related issue of access concerns overseas military ballots. Congress in 1998 passed a law facilitating such voting, but the National Commission on Federal Election Reform (2001) recommends that state handling of military ballots be further regularized by changes in the law. In this case, the argument for a strong national role seems clear cut, in order to facilitate turnout and accountability in elections (7).

Finally, a large battle remains to be fought over the future role of the national government in election administration. Members of the National Commission on Federal Election Reform (2001) openly clashed over how much money and regulatory authority should be forthcoming from the national government. Though a majority of members merely favored a series of recommendations to states, some Democratic members wanted to go farther. Members Leon Panetta, Deval Patrick, Bill Richardson, Kathleen Sullivan, and John Siegenthaler recommended federal mandates for states through setting maximum permissible error limits in voting technologies, requiring provisional voting at polling places, insisting that states purchase voting technologies to make voting more accessible to people speaking differing languages and suffering from physical disabilities, and requiring that states provide every voter with a sample ballot and information on voting procedures before elections (80–81). What should be the proper role of the federal government—as facilitator or regulator of state balloting procedures?

After lengthy negotiations over the 2002 election reform bill, the House and Senate adopted a common position on many of these controversies.

They decided to institute new federal requirements for statewide voter registration systems, provisional balloting, and the handling of disputed ballots. They also agreed to create a new federal commission to assist states and localities with election administration. The House and Senate further decided to give states funds to meet these new standards. Several states also improved their election systems before Congress acted. By mid-2002, fourteen states had improved their procedures for counting votes, and at least fifteen states had revised their recount procedures (Nather 2002, 2035).

Election administration may at first blush seem dull, but it shapes the stability, accountability, and turnout of America's electoral system. Its operations also indirectly affect governmental deliberation by influencing who is elected to direct the government's course. Political debate over how elections operate is sure to persist in coming years because the election of 2000 abundantly displayed the importance of election operations to the political elites—officeholders, parties, and interests—for whom elections are so important.

## Who Counts?

The election of the president, Congress, and state legislatures ultimately depends on the census. The U.S. Census Bureau, created by an act of Congress in 1910, determines the national census every ten years. Each new census becomes the basis of two vital processes for allocating political power. One is *apportionment,* the allocation of U.S. House seats (and therefore electoral college votes) among the states according to population. The second is *redistricting,* the drawing of U.S. House and state legislative districts by the state governments. At stake are vital processes affecting governmental accountability and deliberation. Apportionment and redistricting configure the electoral competition that holds office-holders accountable and influences their deliberations over governmental decisions.

In recent years, the decennial census has been the subject of intense debate between those who believe it should literally be a "head count" and others who hold that head counts are imperfect and should be corrected through supplemental survey samples of the population. All this sounds technical, but the political stakes are plain. Republicans tend to support head counts, whereas Democrats prefer sampling adjustments. Each party, of course, stands to benefit from its preferred method. But the argument extends far beyond partisan self-interest.

Defenders of the traditional "head count" approach base their view on the language of the Constitution. Section 2 of the Fourteenth Amendment declares that "Representatives shall be apportioned among the several States according to their respective numbers, counting the whole number of persons in each State." Counting "the whole number of persons," opponents of sampling argue, allows only for procedures that actually count all citizens. Congressional Republicans have long feared the results of statistical estimations from sampling. Undercounted citizens tend to be low income and nonwhite, and to support Democrats. Including them in the count makes Democratic districts smaller and shifts more Democratic votes into districts that otherwise might elect Republicans. Persons counted more than once, however, usually have more than one residence and tend to vote Republican. Reducing overcounting through sampling adjustment would depopulate some Republican areas and place more Democratic voters in districts including those GOP areas (Monmonier 2001, 122). And is statistical sampling that reliable? Republicans also can point to mistakes in a sample-based statistical adjustment to the census in 1990 that would have erroneously moved a House seat from Wisconsin to Arizona (Anderson and Fienberg 1999, 130–51). They conclude that adjustment procedures are not accurate enough to allocate the missed people to particular states and localities. Sampling adjustment threatens the reliability of the census, and in that way hinders the ability of the citizens to hold government accountable for its actions.

Defenders of sampling-based adjustment contend that census head counts always undercount some citizens and overcount others. For example, the 1990 census reported an undercount of 2.1 percent that was even greater among Latino/as and African Americans (Anderson and Fienberg 1999, 124). Though the letter of the Constitution requires the counting of actual persons, the spirit of the document requires the most thorough and accurate count possible with available technology. Proper electoral system accountability requires that there be no de facto racial discrimination due to the shortcomings of the census count. Before the 2000 count commenced, political scientist Kenneth Prewitt (2000), the director of the Bureau of the Census, argued that new adjustment procedures would reliably correct the statistical flaws of 1990s sampling adjustment methodology.

## TO COURT

Given the intense partisan stakes in the census, it is hardly surprising that the president, Congress, and federal courts became involved in extended scraps about the 1990 and 2000 counts. The Democratic Congress of the late 1980s advocated sampling adjustment, but the first Bush administration strongly objected. The commerce secretary refused to adjust the raw count and arguments over his power to do so landed in federal court. The district court judge in July 1991 upheld the secretary's legal authority to accept only the head count. In a stunning reversal, the circuit court of appeals vacated this initial decision, holding that the plaintiffs in the original trial had proven that the commerce secretary had not made "an effort to achieve equality as nearly as possible" (*City of New York v. Department of Commerce* 1994, 1131). The U.S. Supreme Court finally decided the matter in 1996. Chief Justice William Rehnquist delivered the majority opinion, which overturned the appeals court. The court held that the commerce secretary's decision "conformed to applicable constitutional and statutory provisions" and decreed that the unadjusted census count would serve as the basis for the 1990 apportionment (*Wisconsin v. City of New York* 1996, 7).

The Court did not preclude the possibility of census adjustments in the future. Moreover, by the time the court ruled on the 1990 census, a pitched battle had already begun over the 2000 census methodology. The Census Bureau, now headed by political appointees in a Democratic administration, was as inclined to pursue sampling adjustment as the Republican secretary of commerce had been disinclined ten years earlier. Describing sampling adjustment as "a dagger aimed at the heart of the Republican majority," House Speaker Newt Gingrich (R-Ga.) and other congressional Republican leaders threatened to withhold funding for the Census Bureau unless Democrats agreed to scrap sampling (Broder 1997, A12). In the spring of 1997, they attached a provision barring sampling adjustment to a "must pass" flood relief bill, thinking President Clinton would sign it. Instead, he vetoed the bill and put Republicans on the defensive for playing politics with emergency relief legislation. After another presidential veto threat in November 1997, the combatants struck a compromise. White House lawyers would contest sampling adjustment in federal court, whereas census officials would plan for two different censuses—one with the traditional head count and one with sampling adjustment (Holmes 1997, A12).

The Supreme Court again entered the census fray with a ruling on January 25, 1999. The 5–4 decision ruled on the correct intent of Congress in its passage of the Census Act. According to the court, the act "prohibits the proposed uses of statistical sampling for purposes of apportionment," the allocation of House seats to states. However, the act did allow sampling to be used for other census purposes, including redistricting and allocation of federal funds. The Court also held that the commerce secretary has "substantial authority to determine the manner in which the decennial census is conducted" (*Department of Commerce v. House of Representatives* 1999, 819–20). Republicans hailed the apportionment ruling, but Democrats applauded the court's approval of sampling adjustment in some circumstances. Jousting between Congress and the administration continued over sampling adjustment, with Republican lawmakers contemplating budget cuts and aggressive oversight to constrain the Census Bureau. However, the election of 2000 changed all that. The commerce secretary of the second Bush administration, like that of the first, declared that only the "head count" would determine the 2001–2002 apportionment and redistricting (Armas 2001, 1). So it has.

Taking a census is a technical process, but it will never be free of politics, because the census lies at the heart of America's electoral system. How we count citizens determines the structure of accountability for state, local, and national governments. The intense partisanship surrounding the census creates a political turf war over a crucial aspect of governmental accountability. Parties have many uses in our electoral system, but it is hard to defend their role in census taking. Many states give redistricting authority to nonpartisan or bipartisan commissions, and the quality of our census would probably improve through a similar reform.

## THE ORIGINS OF RACIAL DISTRICTS

Another hot redistricting issue of recent years concerns the question of whether U.S. House districts should be drawn along racial lines. African Americans and Latino/as have long been victims of racial discrimination, and racial districts are a possible way of redressing that disadvantage. The conventional standard for racial districting, passed into law in 1982 by Congress as an amendment to the Voting Rights Act, requires that the percentage of African Americans and Latino/as in a state's U.S. House delegation should be proportional to the percentage of those groups in the state populations as a whole. The drawing of racial districts began with the

1990 census, and state legislatures and federal courts were abuzz with redistricting matters throughout the decade. Repeated challenges to the districts produced court decisions requiring that districts be redrawn. The drawing of racial districts, like census-taking, is an intensely partisan issue that has consumed political elites.

An accountable electoral system allows individual votes to count equally when popular verdicts are passed on elected governments. Federal courts have long held that U.S. House districts must have equal populations within states, but the art of line drawing allows a multitude of ways to devise those equal districts. An electoral system encourages governmental deliberation by creating situations in which public sentiments will be "refined and enlarged," in Madison's phrase. Racial districts, according to their supporters, fulfill this function well by broadening congressional discussions to include more voices from groups that have suffered systematic underrepresentation in the past. However, is this accommodation fair to all voters?

Creation of racial districts followed several decades of actions by Congress and the federal courts to increase national control over the redistricting process. Congress did structure House elections in important ways before this recent spurt of activity, mandating single-member districts in 1842 and population equality of districts in 1872 and requiring districts to comprise a "compact territory" in 1901. A new era of expanded federal involvement began with several Supreme Court decisions in the 1960s. In *Baker v. Carr*, the Court ruled it had jurisdiction over malapportioned state legislative districts. Tennessee's Senate had not been redistricted since 1901, resulting in a gross underrepresentation of urban residents. The court ordered the state of Tennessee to redraw its state senate districts so that they were equal in population. The court ruled similarly regarding the Alabama state legislature in *Reynolds v. Sims* , in 1964. Also that year, in *Wesberry v. Sanders*, the Court held that U.S. House districts must be equal in population in overturning Georgia's districts, some of which were three times the population of others. Several standards emerged from these cases to guide future legislative redistricting. Districts had to have populations very close to mathematical equality. Also, districts must be geographically compact and contiguous, and respect preexisting political subdivisions to the extent practicable.

The Voting Rights Act of 1965 addressed the problem of states and localities drawing districts that deliberately diluted the power of racial minorities. Nine states and parts of seven others with a history of such bias were required to "preclear" any changes in election operations with the U.S. Justice Department. The 1965 act held that "districting arrangements could be found unconstitutional only if they were intentionally drawn to dilute the votes of disadvantaged minorities" (Butler and Cain 1992, 36). Congress changed this standard and allowed the creation of racial districts in its 1982 amendments to the Voting Rights Act. Intent to discriminate need no longer be proved to rule district lines unconstitutional. The new standard held that districting plans that merely had the effect of diluting minority votes were prohibited. In *Thornburg v. Gingles* in 1986, regarding state legislative districts in North Carolina, the Court laid out the three main criteria for determining violations of the 1982 "effects" standard. Courts should find violations in situations involving a minority group that is politically cohesive, has a history of racially polarized voting against it, and is sufficiently large, cohesive, and compact to form a majority in the district.

State legislatures in the early 1990s set about the task of creating racial districts. The national Republican Party pressed for racial districts with strong majorities of African Americans and Latino/as. The partisan logic was straightforward—by "packing" these heavily Democratic voters in a few districts, the electoral prospects for Republicans would grow in other districts. Court challenges came quickly. Aggrieved white voters in states with new racial districts argued in federal court that they were denied the "equal protection of the laws" guaranteed by the Fourteenth Amendment by racial districts drawn solely on the basis of race in ways that violated traditional redistricting principles of compactness, contiguity, and respect for preexisting political subdivisions.

The Supreme Court agreed in *Shaw v. Reno* (1993). Writing for a 5–4 majority, Justice Sandra Day O'Connor argued that the challenged North Carolina districting plan "bears an uncomfortable resemblance to political apartheid. It reinforces the perception that members of the same racial group . . . think alike, share the same political interests, and will prefer the same candidates at the polls. We have rejected such perceptions elsewhere as impermissible racial stereotypes" (2827). Declining to rule directly on the boundaries of the districts in question, the court sent the case back to a lower federal court for scrutiny. The Court did not enunciate clear guidelines for racial districts, signaling instead that they and lower federal courts would review challenges to state redistricting plans on a case-by-case basis. In subsequent decisions throughout the 1990s, federal courts required the redrawing of racial districts in Texas, Georgia, Florida, New York, Virginia, and Louisiana.

## NORTH CAROLINA: THE BELLWETHER CASE

North Carolina, the only state required to redraw districts twice by the Supreme Court during the 1990s, is a case that illuminates the complicated politics of racial districts. The Supreme Court's first words about racial districts concern those drawn in North Carolina. The plan questioned by the court in its 1993 *Shaw v. Reno* decision was actually the tenth redistricting scheme considered by the state legislature in 1991 and 1992. An earlier state-approved plan, providing for only one African-American majority district, failed to win clearance from the Justice Department in 1991. Twenty-two percent of North Carolina's citizens are African American, and the Justice Department held that proportionality required two of the state's twelve House districts to have African-American majorities. African Americans were not concentrated into certain areas of the state, however, making it difficult to draw compact districts that respected preexisting political subdivisions.

The legislature passed a revised plan in early 1992, the tenth alternative it had considered. Democrats dominating the process managed to create a second African-American district, but also arranged district lines so that three Republican House incumbents ended up in even safer districts while a fourth was forced into a marginally Democratic district (Canon 1999, 110). To do this, they had to create a bizarrely shaped twelfth district. The district essentially followed Interstate 85 through the state, incorporating African-American towns and residential areas along the way. Hundreds of miles long, the district was no wider than the highway itself in some places. Mickey Michaux, an eventual congressional candidate in the twelfth, claimed that "in some counties a driver could travel down I-85 with his doors open and kill everyone in the congressional district" (quoted in Biskupic 1993, A4). The other African-American–majority district, numbered the first and located in the eastern part of the state, also possessed an exotic shape. Its perimeter was 2,039 miles long and contained nine counties and parts of nineteen others (Canon 1999, 111). African Americans made up 57.3 percent of the first's population and 56.6 percent of the twelfth's (Sellers, Canon, and Schousen 1998, 281).

In *Shaw v. Reno,* Justice O'Connor referred to the twelfth district as "an effort to segregate the races for purposes of voting, without regard for traditional redistricting principles" (1993, 2826) and sent the case back to a lower federal court for a specific remedy. Meanwhile, African-American candidates Melvin Watt and Eva Clayton won elections in the twelfth and first, respectively, in 1992. In the autumn of 1993, a North Carolina federal district court held, subsequent to *Shaw v. Reno,* that though the two new districts did classify voters by race, their shapes were constitutional. The Supreme Court overruled this decision in *Shaw v. Hunt* (1996). Chief Justice Rehnquist, writing for another 5–4 majority, held that the North Carolina plan violated the Fourteenth Amendment's guarantee that no state shall deny all citizens equal protection of the laws because the districts were far from compact (1906). After much wrangling, the state legislature redrew the districts in 1997, making the first a mere 50.1 percent African American and the twelfth only 46 percent African American (*Congressional Quarterly* 1997, 810). Originally, the state lawmakers had planned to reduce the African-American population proportions even further, but state African-American leaders strongly protested. Throughout these controversies, Watt and Clayton continued to win reelection by comfortable margins.

Opponents of racial districts, convinced that employing race as a criterion for redistricting was an unconstitutional violation of equal protection of the laws—a sort of racial quota employed in redistricting—mounted another challenge in the federal courts. They achieved initial success when a three-judge federal panel ruled against the 1997 remapping (Greenhouse 1999, A14). In May 1999, a unanimous Supreme Court overturned that decision. Justice Clarence Thomas in the majority opinion asserted that "Evidence that blacks constitute even a supermajority in one congressional district will not, by itself, suffice to prove that a jurisdiction was motivated by race in drawing its district lines" (*Hunt v. Cromartie* 1999, 1551).

The court battles continued. A federal district court in early 2000 again voided the 1997 lines, finding that the state legislature was motivated by race, not partisanship, when drawing them. The state appealed again, hoping to finally get the Supreme Court to enunciate clear, comprehensive standards to guide racial districting. Instead, they received a decision very similar to that of 1999. Justice Stephen G. Breyer, writing for the majority, argued that "the party attacking the legislatively drawn boundaries must show at least the legislature could have achieved its legitimate political objectives in alternative ways that are consistent with traditional districting principles" (Caputo and Naresh 2001, 1971).

So stands current law on racial districting. The courts accept partisan motivations for districting, as long as compactness, contiguity and preexisting political subdivisions are reasonably respected in the process. Racial districting often correlates with partisan motivations, because African Americans overwhelmingly vote Democratic. As long as districts adequately respect the principles of compactness, contiguity, and acknowledgment of preexisting political subdivisions, racial districts, like partisan districts, are acceptable. This general doctrine, however, will continue to involve federal court decisions on the legality of particular racial district plans for the near future.

## A REPUBLICAN BOON

Racial districts produced one major and ironic consequence. As Republicans had hoped, the "packing" of African-American voters into racial districts helped Republicans gain control of the U.S. House in 1995, for the first time in forty years. Such an historic change resulted from several factors, including an election environment uniquely favoring Republicans and many districts with incumbents facing relatively new constituents (Petrocik and Desposato 1998). Estimates of Democratic seat losses due to racial districts range from one (National Association for the Advancement of Colored People 1994) to between seven and eleven (Lublin 1997, 114) or twelve (Swain 1993, 78–83). Nationwide, racial districting "turned a number of safe Democratic seats into marginal or Republican-leaning districts," particularly penalizing white Democratic incumbents (Sellers, Canon, and Schousen 1998, 288).

Even if the effects are small, they contributed mightily if not conclusively to Republican control of the House. House election results since 1995 have produced a remarkably close balance between Democratic and Republican seats. The GOP majority was at its highest in 1995 at seventeen seats. In recent elections, the Republican majority shrank to six in 1998 and five in 2000. (It should be noted that these majorities are "effective working majorities," and include not only GOP members, but also a few independents that regularly voted with the GOP.) Assuming the midpoint of the estimated seat loss due to racial districts—about six seats—its likely racial districts prevented Democrats from gaining control of the House in 1998 and 2000. One grand consequence of Republican House control in 1998 was the impeachment of President Clinton in 1999, a near impossibility if Democrats had held even the tiniest House majority. It is difficult to not see racial districts as a small but critical boon to Republicans in the short term, at least.

## For and Against Racial Districts

The Republican boon is reflected in a stream of criticism of racial districts. Packing African Americans into heavily Democratic districts can be an advantage to Republicans in small but significant ways (Swain 1993). Republican control of the House since 1995 seems to bear this point out. It is also possible that racial districts "diminish the overall representation of black interests by reducing the number of sympathetic white Democrats" (Canon 1999, 9). Critics from the left, such as Harvard professor Lani Guinier (1991), argue that racial districts do not promote "authentic" African-American representation. African Americans who win primaries with biracial coalitions in racial districts are less likely to be sincerely evocative of the African-American community's agenda than are those elected with heavily African-American support. Further, even if racial districts produce more minority representatives, legislative institutions remain white-dominated and majoritarian in operation (1476–92). The only lasting solution to the subjugation of racial minorities, to Guinier, lies with creating cumulative voting schemes in multimember districts and providing racial groups formal veto over subsets of policies that disproportionately affect them (1134–54).

Two very different arguments arise from conservatives. First, racial districts disenfranchise white voters. Federal courts have not recognized such harm, though, given the history of racial discrimination in America. Because of that history, race-based white districts have a different meaning than race-based minority districts. A second argument cannot be dismissed so easily. Racial classifications used in districting undermine the goal of a color-blind society (Canon 1999, 5). Such classifications rest upon some notion of "social desert"—that particular groups merit help because of the discrimination they face. But how is the political system supposed to determine this desert and reward the victims? To do this, we need some method that allows us to agree on the magnitude of oppression each group faces. Second, how long do remedial measures remain? Are they permanent? Proponents of racial districts have no answer to this question. Moreover, what if racial districts actually promote segregation, as Representative Henry Hyde (R-Ill.) warns (House of Representatives 1994, 4)? These problems of racial classifications lead conservatives to dispense with them altogether—in affirmative action as well as in racial districting. To them, equal protection means equal treatment of all citizens without regard to racial origin. Violating this principle by defining citizenship by race shatters the accountability of the electoral system to voters as individuals.

Defenders of racial districts point to the legacy of racial discrimination that necessitates them and the promise that increased African-American representation will improve governmental deliberation. "Deliberative democracy recognizes the importance of multiple perspectives and identities within the political process. Representatives of varying races bring perspectives to the legislature that can change agendas and alter preferences" (Canon 1999, 49). In addition to improving deliberation, incorporating previously underrepresented minorities who were long the victims of prejudice can bolster regime legitimacy and stability. In addition, the prospect of electing representatives of one's race after centuries of discrimination could certainly boost turnout, and make the system more accountable to minority interests.

The battle over racial districts will continue as long as race remains controversial in America. And that will probably be a very long time. Parties, interests, and candidates also have a large stake in the effects of racial districts on House election outcomes. Such elite political concern characterizes all of the issues discussed in this chapter. The electoral college, election administration, and census apportionment and redistricting, like racial districts, all shape who wins and loses in the electoral system. The pursuit of electoral victory fuels controversy about all of these issues and accounts for their exalted agenda status despite public inattention to these matters.

However, there is more to these issues than the chase of electoral gain. They have important implications, noted in this chapter, for the turnout, stability, accountability, and deliberation fostered by our electoral system. The stakes may at times seem grubby in battles over these issues, but that is misleading. The core quality of our electoral system is at issue here.

Changing the electoral college can alter our definition of accountability in presidential elections. Should it be a system of federal accountability in which each state decides how to allocate its electoral votes, or one of national accountability in which the nationwide popular vote ultimately dictates the outcome? Though the 2000 election result did not destabilize the political system, the future election of a loser of the popular vote might induce greater political tremors. Decentralized election administration also raises questions of stability and accountability. If the results become untrustworthy in close elections, as they did in Florida in 2000, the legitimacy and potentially the stability of the electoral system suffer.

And accurate voting procedures are essential to keeping elected officials reliably accountable.

Reapportionment and redistricting concern core questions of accountability. Though population equality in redistricting seems essential to the political equality upon which sound accountability is based, the role of race in redistricting remains far more controversial. Is racial representation essential to accountability or does it distort it through a prism of racial difference? Though these four controversies have primarily concerned political elites, their implications are substantial for all citizens. Any rethinking of America's electoral system thus must consider these matters thoroughly. The next chapter invites that rethinking.

CHAPTER 6

# What Sort of Democracy?

The previous chapters exposed more than a few shortcomings of America's electoral system. We need to summarize the most pressing problems thus far identified and consider how to alleviate them. Reform is needed, but not all currently voguish reforms touted as surefire solutions will in fact improve the situation. It is first necessary to identify what is wrong with some current reform alternatives before one can find reforms that might actually do some good. This chapter develops an approach that creates more stability, accountability, turnout, and deliberation in American politics than do present electoral arrangements. However, achieving this requires thinking that differs substantially from the current "reform consensus" in Washington, D.C. It is to the shortcomings of that mindset that we next turn.

## THE REFORMIST CONVENTIONAL WISDOM

Just about every member of Congress finds America's electoral system in need of some sort of reform. Moreover, they are egged on by a bevy of reform groups, such as Common Cause, the Center for Public Integrity, and the League of Women Voters. Discussions of electoral reform in most states also reflects this legislative receptivity and reformist group activism. The reformist consensus in Washington, D.C., and most state capitals is rooted in the Progressive mindset: antiparty, hostile to money in politics, seeking "professionalism" in politics. The media enthusiastically trumpet this conventional wisdom, sharing "the ideology of Progressivism," reacting "viscerally and emotionally" to the role of money in politics (Rosenthal

1998, 105). Increasingly, reformers also tout a Populist-style direct rule by the people as a substitute for corrupt legislative politics (Cain and Miller 2001).

It follows that low electoral turnout, a distinctive and disturbing American problem, does not rank near the top of the current reformist agenda. Instead, campaign finance dominates reform discussions. It so dominates because campaign money offends the Populist desire for political equality and obstructs majority rule through the deployment of cash. Money in politics also impedes the Progressive quest for honest and professional government. It fuels reformers' long-held suspicion of political parties and interest groups. Campaign finance reform's goal is "to limit contributions from dubious sources and to promote a fair and relatively equal fight between major candidates" (Pomper 1997, 1). By curbing the role of money in politics, current reformers hope to make the government accountable to citizens, not just the subset of contributors. In doing so, governmental deliberation will be less tainted by corruption. This supposedly will boost stability by restoring governmental legitimacy in the eyes of many citizens. But will it make much difference in electoral turnout? At most only indirectly, if the public comes to revere their government more once the corruption is removed.

## THE RISE OF CAMPAIGN REGULATION

The Federal Election Campaign Act of 1971 and subsequent FECA amendments in 1974 epitomize this reformist view. The laws imposed a comprehensive system of campaign finance regulation and disclosure upon congressional and presidential candidates that still organizes national campaign finance. Individual candidates, not the parties, stand at the center of the regulatory system. All congressional candidates must disclose all their receipts and expenditures to the bipartisan Federal Elections Commission (FEC). Candidates could receive a maximum of $1,000 per election from individuals (meaning a maximum annual total of $2,000–1,000 each for the primary and general election). A 2002 campaign finance law doubled these limits and indexed them for inflation in future years. Interest groups have to form federally regulated political action committees (PACs) in order to contribute. PACs also must submit complete annual reports to the FEC detailing their receipts and expenditures. PACs can contribute $5,000 per candidate per election, totaling a maximum of $10,000 per candidate in an election year.

Candidates seeking a major party's presidential nomination can raise unlimited private amounts subject to the above rules, or they can opt for partial public financing. A candidate must first raise $5,000 in each of twenty states in order to become eligible for public funds. After that, candidates receive a federal match of up to $250 for each individual contribution to the campaign. PAC contributions are not matched. In return for the federal money, candidates are limited in the amount they can spend in the nomination battle overall ($40.53 million in 2000) and in each state. In the general election, nominees of the two major parties can either choose public financing (equal to $67.56 million in 2000) or raise unlimited funds in federally regulated amounts. Third-party candidates only qualify for federal funds retroactively. If they receive at least 5 percent of the vote in the November election, they then receive public funds equal to their proportion of the average percentage achieved by the two major party candidates.

The rules reflect the Progressive disdain for political parties by sharply limiting parties' financial role in federal elections. The 1974 law initially limited political party spending on behalf of their presidential candidates to only $0.02 per voter. Though indexed for inflation, it still amounts to a small fraction of what candidates legally spend. Further, individual contributions to party committees, previously unlimited, were limited to $20,000 per year with no allowance for inflation. Parties also initially could contribute only as much as an individual PAC could to their congressional candidates, causing party contributions to candidates to plummet while PAC contributions soared (Sabato 1984, 277).

The Supreme Court in *Buckley v. Valeo* (1976) further complicated the campaign finance rules. The Court struck down two other FECA limits—one on campaign spending by candidates and another on "independent expenditures" by PACs—arguing that both are protected First Amendment activities. When PACs spend "independently," as they do in many congressional and presidential campaigns, they do so without formal co-ordination with the campaign of the candidates whom they seek to assist. Under current law, then, congressional candidates face no limit on their spending totals, wealthy candidates can spend unlimited personal funds, and PACs face no similar limit on their independent campaign spending.

The rise of PACs made them a primary target of campaign finance reformers in the 1980s and early 1990s. Proposals to limit or abolish PAC contributions to candidates appeared in Congress annually. Reformers viewed the growth of PAC contributions and campaign spending in the 1980s "as evidence that corrupt practices are a growing problem in the

United States" (Ansolabehere, Gerber, and Snyder 2001, 26). Kenneth R. Mayer (2001) characterizes the reformist view in terms of a syllogism: "Major premise: Interest groups lobby and contribute money to Congress. Minor premise: Congress makes legislative decisions. Conclusion: All legislative decisions are based solely on interest group contributions and lobbying." (72). Political science research during this period found no conclusive evidence that interest group contributions decisively influenced major congressional actions (Wawro 2001, 576–78; Lubenow 2001, vii; Ornstein 2001, 151). Their findings instead suggest that PAC contributions often do give individuals and PACs access to legislators or their staffs, but access falls far short of decisive influence over legislative outcomes. As political scientist Frank Sorauf (1992) noted, access is relatively cheap, but influence is expensive (72). Legislators respond favorably to requests for meetings from contributors, but evidence that contributions determine lawmakers' votes is hard to find. Leaders of reform interest groups and media reporters sympathetic to reform, however, ignored this evidence because it flatly contradicted their Progressive worldview (Ornstein 2001, 151). Given the high cost of campaigns (averaging over a half million dollars in House races and millions in Senate races) and the low aggregate limits on contributions by PACs and individuals ($10,000 and $4,000 respectively combined for primary and general elections), preferential access for contributors is not surprising. The irony is that by limiting contributions, reformers forced incumbent lawmakers to spend more of their time chasing campaign cash.

## THE NEW LOOPHOLES

Major reforms of campaign finance did not occur during this period because incumbent lawmakers, as election winners the beneficiaries of the system, did not perceive a need to move beyond lip service for the reforms. The two congressional parties differed on the sorts of reforms needed, and they and the president placed campaign finance reform low on their agendas. One important change in campaign finance law, however, did occur in the late 1970s. Chafing under the restraints imposed by law, political parties asked the FEC to increase the financial role parties could play in elections. Specifically, the FEC allowed national and state party committees to raise and spend unlimited amounts in "election related activities," such as bumper stickers and get-out-the-vote efforts, at state and local levels (Corrado 1997, 171–72). Unlike the "hard money" limits imposed by the FECA law, this created "soft money" for parties in that it has no legal limits, though it must be reported to the FEC.

In the mid-1990s, the FEC allowed parties to use soft money to fund advertisements on behalf of their candidates. This led to an explosion of "issue advocacy" advertising that touted or denigrated particular candidates without explicitly mentioning for whom one should vote. Such advertisements usually offered no reference to party labels. Unlimited spending on such advertisements was legal in elections despite the hard money limits on party spending because the advertisements did not "expressly advocate" election of a particular candidate (Potter 1997, 227). Interested money gushed through the soft money loophole. In 2000, total soft money contributions to the two major parties exceeded $500 million, a significant increase over 1996 soft money spending (Dudley and Gitelson 2002, 70).

Interest groups have also exploited the "issue advocacy" loophole in recent years. Recall that the *Buckley* decision gave PACs the ability to spend unlimited amounts in "independent expenditures" for campaign advertisements. However, independent expenditures confront two other limits. First, they must be funded through hard money contributions to PACs, which are limited to $5,000 per calendar year. Second, all such contributions must be publicly reported to the FEC. "Issue advocacy" advertising, in which a group or party discusses issues and does not expressly advocate the election or defeat of a particular candidate (through use of words like "support" or "defeat"), is unlimited and unreported.

The Supreme Court views this as legitimate expression of free speech, protected by the First Amendment, and in recent years groups have flooded the airwaves with issue advertisements at election time. It is possible to run effective advertisements showing the shortcomings of a candidate without also explicitly demanding her/his defeat. A common format involves stating unflattering facts about a candidate's issue positions, followed by an appeal to call the candidate's office, complete with telephone numbers. The explosion of issue advocacy advertisements began during the 1996 election cycle, as parties and groups both aggressively exploited this loophole, spending an estimated $135 million (Marcus 1998, 13), a total exceeded in both 1998 and 2000.

## THE CURRENT REFORM CONSENSUS

The rise of issue advocacy and soft money spending, coupled with the persistent PAC role in influencing elected officials through the hard money system, has produced a new reform consensus. The first tenet holds that campaign spending, which has grown in recent years, is out of control and increases corruption in our political system. As money becomes more important, contributors supposedly gain influence at the expense of ordinary citizens. Second, the explosion of spending inhibits the accountability of our electoral system. The influence of money makes officeholders responsive to the money folks, not the broader group of voters. Third, the clutter of advertising during election campaigns, brought on by soft money and issue advocacy loopholes, makes it impossible for voters to determine who is saying what about whom and to hold anyone accountable for the tone and content of the campaign.

Important elements of this consensus do not hold up under empirical scrutiny. Consider two important aspects of the conventional wisdom. First, is campaign spending out of control? Though total campaign spending has grown in recent years, outstripping increases in the Consumer Price Index (CPI), some evidence reveals that reformers' concern about this increase is overstated. Political scientists Stephen Ansolabehere, Alan Gerber, and James Snyder (2001) contend that the proper benchmark for evaluating the increase is the Gross Domestic Product, a measure of the total value of goods and services sold in the economy, not the CPI, a measure of inflation. They argue: "Concerns about corruption, rest on whether we are wasting a large or increasing share of our economy" in efforts to gain access and influence (35). By this measure, they find, we clearly are not, compared to twenty-five years ago. More spending, therefore, does not automatically translate into more corruption, despite what reformers might wish.

Second, is soft money fueling corruption and unaccountable campaigns? Political scientist Ray La Raja (2001) finds that the average "soft money" contribution is far below the level likely to purchase corruption. The median donor gives $500 and the modal (most frequent) contribution is only $250 (103). Given that House races routinely cost at least $500,000 and Senate races several million dollars, it is difficult to become exercised about such small contributions, because they are legal as hard money contributions. It is true, however, that some contributions are extremely large—a few totaling in the millions—prompting justified concerns about corruption. A balanced solution entails capping the maximum allowable amount of soft money contributions, not eliminating them.

One legitimate concern of reformers involves the growth in issue advocacy advertising by interest groups. Recent studies of issue advocacy spending in the 1998 congressional elections revealed a confusing clutter of messages as the election approached (Magleby 2000). In such a situation, it is difficult to determine who is saying what about whom. It remains unlikely, though, that the Supreme Court will reverse itself and allow a ban on such advertising, though many reformers wish for exactly that.

## RECENT REFORMS AND THEIR PROBLEMS

The reform movement triumphed with the passage into law of the McCain-Feingold bill, named after its cosponsors Senator John McCain (R-Ariz.) and Senator Russell Feingold (D-Wisc.), in 2002. The version of McCain-Feingold signed into law by President Bush has four provisions with great implications for elections. First, the law greatly restricts parties from raising or spending soft money. Soft money contributions are limited to $10,000 a year and can only be raised by state and local party organizations and used for "voter registration and other party-building activities affecting federal candidates" ("Some Winners" 2002, 1). Second, the law restricts the ability of unions and corporations to run issue advocacy advertisements during the campaign season. They are banned from running such advertisements within thirty days of a primary election and sixty days of a general election. Third, to offset the soft money restrictions, the law raises the hard money limits (federally regulated and disclosed) that individuals can contribute to parties from $5,000 to $10,000. Fourth, the law raises the total amount of hard money contributions that individuals can make in the two years preceding a federal election from $50,000 to $95,000 ("Some Winners" 2002). It remains unclear, however, if the FEC will effectively enforce the new law's provisions.

The argument for the 2002 law holds that eliminating soft money will stem corruption and banning issue advocacy advertisements will eliminate advertising clutter and make election messages more accountable. Issue advocacy advertisements help unions or corporations gain influence over elected officials, and this dubious practice must be halted. Money used in these ways leads to corruption and must be banned. To ensure campaigns are funded adequately, it slightly adjusts the hard money limits to counterbalance the loss of soft money. The law reflects the reformist consensus on the need to eliminate rampant corruption resulting from abuses of America's electoral politics.

The basic premise of the reform, however, is flawed. As research revealed, political money has not grown as a segment of our GDP since

1976, when the FECA regime operated in its pristine form without loopholes. Political science studies do not find widespread abuses of influence due to PAC contributions. Corruption has not obviously grown as a problem. In order to limit this alleged corruption, the 2002 law imposes restrictions on campaign expression. However, as Jeffrey Rosen (2000) notes: "In an era of talk radio and the Internet, there are almost unlimited opportunities for politically engaged citizens to receive and express competing viewpoints on politics. The notion that wealthy voices necessarily drown out poor ones is ... untrue: anyone with a telephone and a modem can educate herself about the candidates and publish her opinions for the world to read" (22). A regulatory regime that seeks to "balance" campaign expression is therefore bound to fail.

The law also directly contradicts the *Buckley* decision on the matter of issue advocacy, making it unlikely the Supreme Court would uphold the ban. In *Buckley,* the court held that "so long as persons and groups eschew expenditures that in express terms advocate the election or defeat of a clearly identified candidate, they are free to spend as much as they want to promote the candidate and his views" (Kelly 2001, 1). And will the reform really limit money in electoral politics? Sociologist Paul Starr (1998) thinks not: "The most likely effect is simply to divert spending from political parties to unregulated activity by advocacy groups—that is, to bring about a change in the organizational form of uncontrolled spending, not to control it" (4).

As Starr suggests, the 2002 law is a profoundly antiparty reform that dramatically reduces the role of parties in electoral politics by depriving them of most of their current financial resources. Its attempt to regulate interest group spending on advertising, however, seems likely to fail in the courts, leaving its net effect one of boosting the role of interest groups in electoral politics at the expense of parties. This is exactly what the Progressive reforms of the early twentieth century accomplished. The 2002 law is the latest attempt to remove corruption from politics by punishing parties. Sadly, the empirical assumptions behind the effort are deeply flawed. It is not obvious that corruption has grown. Empowering interest groups in election campaigns at the expense of parties is hardly likely to make election messages more accountable. Given that most soft-money contributions are small, it is surely possible to remove the egregious contributions by instituting a soft money contribution limit that would not shrivel the party role in elections. A limit of, say, $50,000 on soft money contributions, without restriction on how parties can spend the funds, would keep parties in the game while curbing the potentially corrupting influence of large contributions.

The law passed because it struck an unholy alliance between the electoral self-interest of incumbents and the reformers' agenda. Curtailing soft money helps incumbents because much of that money has funded challengers who must spend big to overcome the name recognition advantage of incumbents. In addition, a provision in the Senate version lowering television advertising rates during elections was struck from the bill in the House. Maintaining high advertising rates disadvantages challengers because they usually have fewer funds to pay for expensive advertisements. The law overall makes fundraising more difficult by abolishing soft money contributions but does nothing to lower the costs of campaigns. This gives incumbents an advantage with their larger campaign treasuries and fundraising networks.

More ambitious proposals, long advocated by reform groups like Common Cause and Public Citizen, involve public financing of federal and state elections (Sabato 1989, 56–65). Some proposals provide total public funding for candidates in return for their agreeing to expenditure limits. Others, such as Maine's financing law, give candidates public matching of small private contributions in return for an overall spending limit. Any public plans must be voluntary, because *Buckley* upheld the right of individual candidates to spend unlimited amounts of their own funds. The public plans, however, cannot eliminate interest group spending without conflicting with *Buckley*. In addition, most public finance schemes are candidate-centered in that they sharply limit the money parties can raise and employ in elections. They operate on the assumption that too much money abounds in elections, and that we must curtail such actual or potential corruption. Like the 2002 law, they chase the old Progressive dream of elections free of strong parties and interested money.

This dream is not one worth pursuing. It is both unrealistic and undesirable. In just about every other constitutional democracy, parties stand at the center of electoral politics, and facilitate accountable elections and coherent results. Further, the total amount of campaign spending is not a great problem, as Ansolabehere, Gerber, and Snyder (2001) note. What is a problem is the way the money is spent. Campaigns narrowly seek to activate targeted groups of likely voters (Schier 2000). Neither incumbents nor challengers find it rational to allocate their resources to expand the electorate. Instead, each uses campaign technologies to persuade that small group of persuadable likely voters.

Infrequent electoral competitiveness is another big problem. The top spender usually wins in congressional elections, and only some 35 of 435 House contests in 2000 featured truly competitive races. Gary Jacobson (1997) found that the essential variable influencing the outcome of House elections was the amount of the challenger's spending. Campaign finance reformers are right to stress the need for more competitive elections, and this can only occur if challengers in congressional contests are more equitably funded. Limiting the amount of permissible campaign money and the means for raising it hurts challengers, who have more trouble raising funds than do incumbents. Reformers need to obsess less about corruption and focus more on competitiveness and turnout in elections.

### USEFUL CAMPAIGN FINANCE REFORM

Examining the experience of other constitutional democracies can impart some useful lessons about proper campaign finance goals. Many long-established democratic nations do partially or fully publicly finance elections, but with the exception of Japan and the United States, the public money goes *to the parties* to spend as they wish (Semetko 1996). This feature alone makes elections party-centric and would cut the "clutter" of messages that individualistic candidates employ to swamp the American airwaves. America is the only constitutional democracy in the world with the following combination of election laws: financing centered on candidates, not parties; no free public airtime to parties or candidates; no public subsidies to national legislative candidates and no campaign spending limits. The result is our confusing electoral free-for-all.

If we wish our electoral system to more consistently promote stability, high turnout, accountability, and governmental deliberation, we need more competitive, transparent, and inclusive elections. Requiring that all issue advocacy spending be instantaneously disclosed will aid transparency. Offering parties free blocks of airtime will cut the demand for money that fuels fundraising and contributes to noncompetitive races dominated by incumbents. If soft money must go, hard money limits for contributions by individuals and PACs to parties should rise to, for example, $50,000 to place parties at the center of electoral finance. Party-based elections are more likely to involve coherent teams of players rather than our individualistic and cluttered campaigns. And making election funding more party-centered allows parties to function as a useful "buffer" between elected officials and interested money (Sabato 1989, 35–38). Contrary to the Progressive conventional wisdom, party-centered finance can help to reduce the likelihood of corrupt influence by moneyed interests upon elected officials.

## THE TURNOUT PROBLEM

Making elections inclusive requires broad-based messages from candidates and parties as well as high turnouts that reward such messages. But here we have a chicken-and-egg problem. Candidates and parties have little incentive to broaden their outreach, given the low probability that turnout will consequently rise to benefit them. After all, turnout has slumped for decades, and it is risky for any campaign to abstain from the targeting of likely voters that is essential for victory. Yet, turnout is unlikely to rise without more broadly targeted messages. This vicious circle can only be changed by structural intervention.

The structural change necessary to boost turnout from America's currently abysmal levels involves lowering the legal barriers to voting. Among established democracies, only the United States and France require individual citizens to register to vote on their own initiative. Political scientists estimate that turning registration into a governmental responsibility, as is the norm among longstanding democracies, would boost turnout between 9 and 14 percent (Wolfinger and Rosenstone 1981; Powell 1986). Creating a national system that requires the government to register all eligible citizens and inform them of their local polling places at election time will boost turnout more than any other single reform. If objections of federalism arise from such nationalization, administration of the system could be delegated to states, subject to national guidelines. If a greater national role in voter registration proves politically impossible, states should adopt Election Day registration. Now in effect in six states, it boosted turnout in those states in 2000 (Committee for the Study of the American Electorate 2001, 10).

Four other possible changes might increase turnout: early voting, mail voting, on-demand absentee voting, and creating an Election Day holiday. None of them, however, are likely to boost turnout as much as would comprehensive national registration. In early voting, the polls open as much as twenty-one days before Election Day. Thirteen states now employ it, with no clear benefit to turnout (Caltech 2001, 39; Committee for the Study of the American Electorate 2001, 9). A recent cross-national study finds no boost to turnout by an increase in the number of polling days

(Franklin 1996, 227–28). Similarly, Oregon's experiment with mail voting has yet to demonstrate a distinctively positive effect on turnout, though postal voting has boosted turnout in other countries (Committee for the Study of the American Electorate 2001, 10; Franklin 1996, 227; Caltech 2001, 39). Allowing citizens to vote absentee at their request, like mail voting, increases convenience for established voters but does not bring "many non-voters to the polls" (Caltech 2001, 39). It is difficult to assess the impact of an Election Day holiday on turnout. Sunday voting seems to boost turnout in other democracies, and declaring a holiday for balloting may have a comparable effect in the United States (Franklin 1996, 227).

The problem of election administration remains an important one. The reform commissions that reported recommendations of election administration in 2001 tended to agree on a variety of necessary changes. These included improving election equipment, creating uniform vote counting procedures, computerizing voter registration lists, hiring more poll workers, ensuring an adequate number of polling places, and allowing provisional ballots for people not listed as registered but who possibly should be on the list. Instead of leaving important vote standards to variable definition by the states, the national government should create in law minimum standards for states to meet in administering elections, supplemented by federal grants to assist them in meeting the standards. The standards should include maximum permissible error limits for voting technologies, requiring provisional voting, mandating the use of technologies that are most accessible, and providing every voter with a sample ballot and information on voting procedures. Election Day operations should not be compromised by the vagaries of federalism, and national standards can prevent this from happening. The House and Senate agreed on many of these improvements when writing their election administration reform bill in 2002.

Fairness also requires an end to partisanship in redistricting and apportionment. Decennial reapportionment should not be a partisan affair, but instead be left to nonpartisan redistricting commissions at the national (for apportionment) and state (for redistricting) levels. Popular control of government also will grow if we limit the number of choices that confront voters on their ballots. I could not make sense of most of my twenty-six choices in 2000, voting reliably only in nine contests. We should be able to reduce the number of choices on every general election ballot to ten or less. Abolishing initiatives would help, as would making more offices appointive, not elective. If a president can appoint his attorney general, why can't a governor? Americans also are called to vote too often. National, state, and local elections need to be consolidated around a single Election Day every year. Local election turnouts of 10 to 20 percent are abysmal by any standard and result from too-frequent elections.

## Toward Proportional Representation?

A more fundamental debate about America's electoral system goes far beyond Election Day mechanics. Proponents of proportional representation (PR) find it superior to the single-member, simple plurality system currently employed in American elections. Proponents of PR claim its superiority in providing "fairness and responsiveness" (Blais and Massicotte 1996, 74). PR is supposedly fairer in that it provides each party a proportion of legislative seats commensurate with its share of the vote. Single-member plurality systems (SMP), in contrast, offer no such guarantees. PR also allows more responsiveness to the diversity of opinions among the citizenry, whereas SMP often marginalizes minority opinions. SMP advocates, in response, tout the superior governmental stability resulting from SMP systems that regularly deliver responsibility for governing into the hands of one party that wins a majority of seats. This streamlined authority also provides superior accountability in that voters know which party is responsible for governmental outcomes. PR, they counter, often produces unstable and complex coalition governments. Voters cannot fathom the consequences of their votes, because ruling governmental coalitions result from elite bargaining among several parties after the election. Under such circumstances, it is hard to hold the government accountable at election time.

PR is unlikely to become a feature of American elections anytime soon. David Farrell (2001) identifies four reasons why. First, despite widespread acknowledgment by Americans of shortcomings in their electoral system, particularly since the 2000 election, there is no groundswell for basic change in electoral structure. Second, the frequency of "divided" government prevents Americans from taking exception to the shortcomings of one-party rule. Third, the competitive balance of the two-party system produces closely proportional overall results. Fourth, party weakness forestalls growing hostility to "party rule" such as resulted during the Progressive era (42–43). Of these reasons, the point about proportional results seems strongest: "if only two [major] parties run candidates then even a plurality rule system may operate quite proportionately" (Dunleavy and Margetts 1995, 24).

America's SMP system does provide some perverse incentives. Though national elections produce roughly proportional overall results, millions of votes are "wasted" in uncompetitive district elections. This is the case in U.S. House elections, over 90 percent of which were uncompetitive in 2000. The incentive to vote in uncompetitive elections is low, because it is far from clear that one's vote will really affect the outcome. This contributes to America's chronically low turnouts. It is true that other SMP countries have higher turnouts than does the United States, but most nations with high turnouts have some explicit forms of proportionality built into their systems. A recent study of turnout in twenty-nine established democracies found that proportionality in election outcomes contributes positively to turnout, when one controls for other factors (Franklin 1996, 227).

As noted in chapter 2, though, PR in the United States may be undesirable as well as infeasible. Our diverse nation could easily produce myriad parties in national and state legislatures under PR, creating a complex politics in which accountability and governmental stability suffer greatly. What is needed is an electoral system that facilitates the four goals mentioned early in the book—stability, accountability, high turnout, and deliberation. Both PR and SMP systems fall short, with PR sacrificing governmental stability and accountability and SMP discouraging turnout and party-based deliberation. The preferable alternative is the single transferable vote, or STV. Under STV in a single-member district system, voters rank order their preferences and the lowest first-place finishers are eliminated and their ballots reallocated among the other candidates until one candidate gets a majority in a single-member district. Advocates appropriately call this an "instant runoff" system: "Instant runoff voting simulates a series of runoff elections, but in a single round of voting that corrects the flaws of plurality voting—the spoiler problem and the lack of majority rule—and runoff elections—having to pay for two elections" (Ritchie, Hill, and Kleppner 2000, 36). The result of the "instant runoff" is a single-member majority (SMM) system similar to the one used in Australia.

The STV-SMM system is clearly consistent with high turnouts. The nation with the world's highest turnouts, Malta, uses STV. The second or possibly even the third choice of every voter may end up deciding the election. Given this, parties and candidates must address the electorate more broadly and cannot narrowly focus on the first preferences of a small group of undecided voters, as they currently do in American elections (Schier 2000, 212–13). Parties have an incentive to contact more voters under STV-SMM than they currently do, and that can only help turnout. STV-SMM also broadens the available choices for voters by allowing them to cast a first choice consistent with their wishes while perhaps casting a second choice for a candidate more likely to win. STV-SMM bolsters governmental stability, by giving every winner a majority of the vote, and giving an advantage to the two major parties that are most likely to end up as the first or second choices of most voters. Results are likely to be decisive, and one-party majority governments as regularly occur in Ireland and Malta, the two nations employing the STV-SMM in national elections.

STV-SMM may seem an unnecessary complication of an already baroque electoral system, but it promises to deliver greater governmental stability and accountability than PR systems while stimulating higher turnouts and producing more representative results than our current SMP system. STV-SMM also will further these goals in presidential elections. STV-SMM could be grafted onto the electoral college system in one of two ways. Despite the 2000 election controversy, the electoral college seems destined to remain in the Constitution indefinitely. Given this, we could adopt instant runoff voting at either the statewide level or at the congressional district level for allocating electoral votes. I personally prefer a district-level allocation of electoral votes, with two additional votes going to the statewide winner. That would help to make our elections more party-based, with House and presidential candidates gaining an increased incentive to campaign side-by-side and harmonize their programs. Making American elections more party-based makes accountability easier and encourages party-based deliberation in government, a form of decision making likely to be much superior to the one used by individualistic legislators who constantly run scared in our current system. An STV-SMM system will broaden the discourse of our electoral politics, produce stable and party-based governments that collectively deliberate over policy, making it easier for harried voters to know whom to hold accountable for governmental actions.

## What Sort of Democracy?

What sort of democracy is implicit in the reforms I advocate? My approach begins with a sober realization of the limited knowledge and interest most citizens have in politics. Responsiveness cannot be a useful goal for America's electoral system because the public has limited issue knowledge that can serve as a basis for enforcing responsiveness. Given an uninterested and uninformed public frequently possessing inconsistent policy preferences, elections cannot really function as exercises in public issue deliberation. The many shortcomings of the initiative process identified in chapter 5 reveal the folly of demanding too much time and attention from voters for such matters. Social choice theory exposes the futility of defining elections as "meaningful" expressions of the public's policy preferences (Riker 1982, 235–39, 244–50). Elections do not make policy; they elect leaders to deliberate over policy on our behalf. An electoral system must provide voters an effective method for holding these leaders accountable.

The Populist-Progressive vision of the voice of the people ruling is simply a sham. We cannot reliably identify that voice on policy due to public ignorance and the limits of elections as means for making collective policy choices. Realistically, American democracy at its best can resemble Joseph Schumpeter's conception: a circulation of elites held accountable by a usually inattentive public. Schumpeter (1976) holds that because of the unreality of the political world for most citizens, and their correct view that their vote has little effect on the outcome of an election involving a mass electorate, the average citizen is likely to "expend less disciplined effort on mastering a political problem than he expends on a game of bridge" (261). Given this limitation, we should "make the deciding of issues by the electorate secondary to the election of the men who are to do the deciding" (269). Ideally, the competition involves two teams of leaders, with one winning a stable majority that allows them to govern, so that voters can hold that team accountable at the next election.

Benjamin Barber (1984), a leading proponent of participatory democracy, calls Schumpeter's approach "thin democracy" dominated by representative institutions and elite interest groups. It is a democracy whose procedures are merely "means to exclusively individualistic and private ends," it is "never a politics of transformation ... a politics that conceives women and men at their worst (in order to protect them from themselves), never at their potential best (to help them become better than they are)" (4, 24–25). Barber's aspiration to revise and improve humanity through politics is grand, but his fellow citizens' beliefs and behavior stand in his way. For Barber's vision to become reality, citizens above all must want to improve themselves through politics. In fact, only a small activist segment really aspires to this. Most citizens seek other ways to become "better than they are" and would just as soon delegate politics to others.

Given these realities, it is important to make America's electoral system simple and user-friendly, so that citizens can use it reliably to chose able leaders and hold them accountable for their actions. That is best done by organizing politics around teams of like-minded leaders, called political parties, and creating procedures that facilitate majority victories by a particular team that can be held accountable at the next election. Once elected, the team can deliberate, "refining and enlarging" public views over policy when addressing public problems.

America's electoral system impedes the operation of this vision. Progressivism left America with the legacy of a political system that asks too much of marginally interested citizens and weakens the ability of party teams to coherently operate state and national governments. Parties need to return to the center of American elections. The national government should grant state and national parties large blocks of free television time. That will simultaneously give parties power over both their candidates and election messages and lessen the frenetic money chase by candidates raising cash for television advertising. States should adopt one-punch partisan ballots, making it easier for voters to cast a straight-party vote. Party voting helps less knowledgeable citizens make a coherent set of choices based on simply knowing which team one prefers. Also, we can limit and fully disclose the role of political money without eviscerating parties—by channeling contributions through parties to candidates. All this can make elections better mechanisms of accountability.

We should abandon the overused instruments of direct democracy—particularly the initiative. Chapter 5 explained how initiative voting cannot reliably deliver a coherent public verdict on issues and how initiative politics has become a festival of interest group powerplays. Legislative politics is sometimes unsavory, but it does regularly offer opportunities for serious deliberation over policy. The public can hold lawmakers accountable through elections. Initiatives, however, undercut the deliberative power of legislatures and greatly complicate the ballot. And whom can the public hold accountable for the consequences of an initiative? The voters? The interests backing a successful proposition? The political consultants who made the winning advertisements? There is no regular mechanism for enforcing accountability, even if it were obvious who was responsible for a successful initiative. The public loves the initiative process in states where it exists, but that does not make it a useful weapon of democracy—just another public illusion. Even participatory democrat Benjamin Barber (1984) has little use for contemporary initiatives, holding they "fall easy victim to plebiscitary abuses and the manipulation by money and elites of popular prejudice" (156). Because initiatives undercut elected officials' accountability to voters, governmental stability, legislative deliberation, and do not boost turnout, it is impossible to justify their continued existence. If initiatives cannot be abolished, states should at least minimize their existence by raising the requirements for placing them on the ballot.

Ultimately, Americans are the victims of the reformers who created the nation's current electoral system. The Progressive mindset so much in vogue among the nation's political activists contains a catalogue of errors. Initiatives do not improve democracy. Registration need not be a personal responsibility. Parties are not the root of political evil. Money in politics is neither excessive nor inevitably wicked. Political money instead can encourage turnout in an electoral system that rewards inclusive campaign appeals, such as one employing the single transferable vote. Above all, clean politics need not be as exclusive as America's is now. As E. E. Schattschneider (1977) noted decades ago: "There is nothing hopelessly wrong with the raw materials of politics" (34). Many reformers strongly disagree, and have convinced most of the American public.

The reformers are wrong. Our electoral system will function well if we become realistic about what it can accomplish. Constructive change involves simplifying elections by requiring fewer ballot choices and making our politics more party-based. We can elect teams of leaders, hold them accountable, and in so doing enhance governmental and regime stability. Turnout, the problem reformers tend to ignore, can rise with registration reforms. Party-based finance can channel money to boost turnout and simultaneously curb corruption.

Americans need to rediscover a truth most long-established constitutional democracies never forgot: simple ballots and party-based elections facilitate popular control of government. The experience of Canada, Great Britain, France, and many other democracies illustrates this obvious truth. It's not too late for America to grasp it again. To do that, we need to "get over" our century-long infatuation with the Progressive reforms that created our peculiar democracy. And the time to start is now.

# Less Peculiar

It is not difficult to envision a resolution of the 2000 presidential election less peculiar than that which actually transpired. This final chapter examines how it all might have turned out differently if certain reforms advocated in this book had been in place on election night, 2000. Imagine if the revised election administration procedures advocated in previous chapters had guided the resolution of controversies resulting from 2000's close race for president in the state of Florida.

Fortunately, we do not have to speculate much about what those reforms might have been. Florida adopted a great number of them in an election reform law signed by Governor Jeb Bush in May 2001. The new law prohibits punch-card voting systems and requires counties to adopt optical scan or other possible electronic voting systems that promise more reliability. Florida's counties received $24 million from the state over two years to modernize their voting equipment and $6 million for voter education programs and poll-worker training. The law mandated creation of a centralized voter registration database by June 2002 and provided $2 million to create it. Provisional voting gained adoption, with such votes subject to immediate review by county election officials. The law also clarified procedures for overseas military ballots, created a standard ballot design for the state, and instituted clear and uniform statewide definitions for determining a voter's ballot intent in disputed cases.

In the future, the state will certify vote totals eleven days after the election. The state elections canvassing commission, including the governor and two cabinet members appointed by him or her, will make the final certification. Recounts occur automatically if the vote difference between the two leading candidates is one-half of 1 percent or less. In addition to this automatic recount, a candidate can request an additional recount of all overvotes (ballots marked for two or more candidates) and undervotes (ballots marked for no candidate). All recounts must be complete, however, by the certification deadline. Given the ease of recounting optical-scan votes, this should not prove a problem. ("Governor Signs Historic Election Reform Into Law" 2001, 2; State Senate of Florida 2001).

We shall assume that the reformed Florida system was administered well, as it unfortunately was not during the 2002 Florida Democratic gubernatorial primary. Let us also assume that Congress had passed national standards for election administration similar to those national lawmakers contemplated in 2002. Under this scenario, states had received money to upgrade election equipment, with optical-scan voting systems now the national norm. All states had centralized voter registration databases, better-trained poll workers, common procedures for provisional ballots, more straightforward ballot structures, and clear standards detailing what constituted a legitimate vote. With such procedures in place in Florida and other states, the resolution of the 2000 election would have been much more peaceful and consensual. The following narrative suggests why.

## AN ALTERNATIVE NARRATIVE

Early on election night, it became clear that Al Gore was narrowly winning the large states he needed to achieve an electoral college majority. In addition to winning the vital states of Michigan, Pennsylvania, Illinois, New York, and California, Gore scored a victory in Florida. The networks declared him the victor in Florida immediately after the polls closed. Still, it became clear that Florida was the main hope for George W. Bush to prevail in the electoral college, and his campaign held out hope that the networks were wrong.

They were not. Gore carried Florida in this scenario thanks to improved voting technology. Recall that with optical-scan technology, the number of undervotes and overvotes shrinks. In jurisdictions employing optical-scan technology in 2000, only 1.5 percent of presidential ballots had undetermined content (Caltech 2002, 21–22). In the real Florida of 2000, Gore was one of two candidates selected on 40,371 overvotes, but Bush was a selection on only 15,803 overvotes according to a postelection analysis of statewide overvotes and undervotes. The media consortium undertaking the investigation put the statewide total of overvotes and undervotes at 175,010, or 2.9 percent of all ballots cast (Bousquet and Tobin 2001, 1).

The key to Gore's victory lies in the new voting technologies that would have produced fewer Florida overvotes. Given the actual total overvotes and undervotes, and assuming that 1.5 percent instead of 2.9 percent of Florida ballots had unclear content, the number of overvotes and undervotes would shrink to about 90,500. Of that total, about 58,800 would be overvotes. That means an additional 55,000 disqualified overvotes might well have been counted using the more reliable voting technology. Of that total, given the actual 2000 proportions, Gore could be expected to receive about 20,850 extra votes to Bush's 8,160. That translates into a Gore victory margin statewide of about 12,700 votes.

However, the actual Gore margin could have been bigger. A group of political scientists estimate that Gore also lost at least 2,000 additional votes in Palm Beach County alone due to incorrect ballot punches for Pat Buchanan, whose name was next to Gore's on the punch card ballot (Wand et al. 2001). Adding another 2,000 votes to Gore's margin improves his Florida vote performance to an estimated 14,700 votes. In fairness, let's also assume that the improved procedures for counting overseas military ballots improves Bush's total by 500 votes and that among all other ballots he finished 537 votes ahead of Gore, as was actually certified by the state. Subtracting these votes from Gore's margin still leaves the vice president ahead by about 13,600 votes statewide.

This admittedly speculative exercise suggests that improved voting technology would likely have produced a Gore victory in Florida by a margin of several thousand votes. How would this have affected election night politics? First, the new Florida law mandates a recount when the margin between candidates is less than one-half of one percent. Therefore, a recount of all duly recorded votes would have occurred. The law also permits a candidate to request a statewide recount of overvotes and undervotes. Would Bush have requested the recount? The new Florida law would have given him until 5 P.M. on the second day after the election to decide.

Recall that by the day after the election, Bush would know he was more than one-half million votes behind in the popular vote. None of his options would have looked promising. It is likely that under reformed national voting processes he would have lost four other states by narrow margins. His actual losses in those states were narrow—Iowa (4,100 votes), Wisconsin (5,700 votes), Oregon (6,700 votes), and New Mexico (400

votes). Why would he still lose them under improved election administration? There is no strong reason to believe the results would have been
overturned in any or all cases, particularly given how the revised Florida
procedures helped Gore. If Bush could have reversed all four of those
narrow losses through recounts and legal appeals, he could have won the
electoral college vote without Florida. That, however, seems the longest of
long shots, particularly under more reliable national voting guidelines.
Those guidelines seemingly foreclosed the Fourteenth Amendment argument that allowed Bush to prevail in *Bush v. Gore*. With uniform national
voting guidelines, state and local variations in election administration that
violate the "equal protection" of all voters become much less likely.

Because a Florida recount had to occur, Bush may well have pressed
for an additional recount of overvotes and undervotes. What did he have
to lose? Perhaps his reputation as a "good loser." More likely, given our
revised circumstances, his loss in the popular vote would cause him to
concede on election night. Albert Gore could confidently claim the presidency on the strength of a victory in the popular vote and electoral college. The election had been a close one, but improved voting procedures
had helped forestall a major political crisis.

## THE BROADER LESSON

The point of all this is that electoral systems have great consequences
for what government does, for the fate of the nation. A Gore presidency
would have pursued many policies differing from those of the Bush
administration. The large tax cuts of 2001 would surely not be law, judicial appointees would have had a different philosophy than do those
appointed by Bush, and the domestic agenda under Gore would have
involved more emphasis on health care and environmental issues. Politically, the national tragedy of September 11, 2001, would have given the
Democrats an historic opportunity to win public approval for their conduct of foreign and defense policy, issue areas in which Republicans had
long been viewed by the public as more competent. The results of the
2000 presidential election arguably produced a major shift in American
politics and public policy.

And guess what? Some peculiar and poorly functioning features of our
electoral system may well have created that major shift in national politics
and policy. The next time you are tempted to dismiss the importance of
America's electoral process, think about that.

# Notes

## Introduction

1. As a result of the recount controversies, Florida reformed its election system, reworking and clarifying the calendar for the "protest" and "contest" phases for possible recounts, upgrading voting technology, and further defining standards for determining a valid vote and for proper election administration.

## Chapter 3

1. My shift from female to male pronouns is intentional here. Though a majority of voters today are female, women did not receive a national guarantee of suffrage until the passage of the Twentieth Amendment to the Constitution in 1919. The electorate in the 1870s and 1880s was restricted to males only. Later in the chapter I explain how the decline in turnout in the early twentieth century predated female suffrage.

2. An additional argument minimizing the problem of nonvoting holds that nonvoters have similar attitudes and candidate preferences to those of voters. Some evidence supports this proposition (Texeira 1992, 97–101), but it assumes that we can trust that nonvoters' survey responses represent stable political attitudes and candidate preferences. That is unlikely, given their very limited knowledge of politics (Zaller 1992; Doppelt and Shearer 1999). Even if we accept that assumption, there is no reason to suppose that the correlation of voter and nonvoter views will hold in future elections.

## Chapter 5

1. See *Cook* v. *Gralike* (2001) on the limits of state power over federal elections.

# References

*ABC News/Washington Post* Poll. 2002, November 12. Retrieved November 13, 2002, at http://pollingreport.com/wh2/post3htm.

Aldrich, John H. 1995. *Why Parties? The Origin and Transformation of Party Politics in America*. Chicago: University of Chicago Press.

Allen, Howard W., and Kay Warren Allen. 1981. "Vote Fraud and the Validity of Election Data." In *Analyzing Electoral History*, edited by Jerome M. Clubb, William H. Flanigan, and Nancy H. Zingale. Beverly Hills, Calif.: Sage Publications.

Anderson, John B. 2000. "Flunk the Electoral College, Pass Instant Runoffs." Washington, D.C.: Center for Voting and Democracy. Typescript.

Anderson, Margo, and Stephen E. Fienberg. 1999. "To Sample or Not to Sample: The 2000 Census Controversy." *Journal of Interdisciplinary History* 30: 1–35.

Ansolabehere, Stephen, Alan Gerber, and James M. Snyder, Jr. 2001. "Corruption and the Growth of Campaign Spending." In *A User's Guide to Campaign Finance Reform*, edited by Gerald C. Lubenow. Lanham, Md.: Rowman and Littlefield.

Armas, Genaro C. 2001, March 2. "Battle Brewing over Census Count." *Associated Press*. Retrieved March 4, 2001, at http://www.aol.com.

Arnold, R. Douglas. 1990. *The Logic of Congressional Action*. New Haven, Conn.: Yale University Press.

Bachrach, Peter. 1967. *The Theory of Democratic Elitism*. Boston: Little, Brown.

*Baker v. Carr.* 1962. 369 U.S. 186.

Barber, Benjamin. 1984. *Strong Democracy: Participatory Politics for a New Age*. Berkeley: University of California Press.

Bennett, Stephen Earl. 2003. *The American Ignoramus*. New York: Peter Lang Publishers.

Berelson, Bernard, Paul F. Lazarsfeld, and William N. McPhee. 1999. "Democratic Practice and Democratic Theory." In *American Government: Readings and Cases*, 13th edition, edited by Peter Woll. New York: Longman.

Bessette, Joseph M. 1994. *The Mild Voice of Reason: Deliberative Democracy and American National Government*. Chicago: University of Chicago Press.

Biskupic, Joan. 1993. "N.C. Case to Pose Test of Racial Redistricting." *Washington Post*, April 20, A4.

Blais, Andre, and Louis Massicotte. 1996. "Electoral Systems." In *Comparing Democracies: Elections and Voting in Global Perspective,* edited by Lawrence LeDuc, Richard G. Niemi, and Pippa Norris. Thousand Oaks, Calif.: Sage Publications.

Blumenthal, Sidney. 1980. *The Permanent Campaign: Inside the World of Elite Political Operatives.* Boston: Beacon Press.

Bousquet, Steve, and Thomas C. Tobin. 2001. "Without Overvotes Gore Was Doomed." *St. Petersburg Times,* November 12, A1.

Bowler, Shaun, Todd Donovan, and Caroline J. Tolbert. 1998. *Citizens as Legislators: Direct Democracy in the United States.* Columbus: Ohio State University Press.

Broder, David. 1997. "GOP Minds Made Up on Census." *Washington Post,* 20 August, A19.

———. 2000. *Democracy Derailed: Initiative Campaigns and the Power of Money.* New York: Harcourt.

*Buckley v. Valeo.* 1976. 96 S. Ct. 612.

Burke, Edmund. [1774] 1999. "Speech to the Electors of Bristol." In *American Government: Readings and Cases,* 13th edition, edited by Peter Woll. New York: Longman.

Burnham, Walter Dean. 1965. "The Changing Shape of the American Electoral Universe." *American Political Science Review* 59: 7–28.

———. 1970. *Critical Elections and the Mainsprings of American Politics.* New York: W. W. Norton.

———. 2002. "Voter Turnout Rates, United States, South and Nonsouth, 1798–1998," in *Vital Statistics on American Politics 1999–2000,* edited by Harold W. Stanley and Richard G. Niemi. Washington, D.C.: Congressional Quarterly Press.

"Bush v. Gore." 2001. In *Bush v. Gore: The Court Cases and the Commentary,* edited by E. J. Dionne and William Kristol. Washington, D.C.: Brookings Institution Press.

Butler, David, and Bruce Cain. 1992. *Congressional Redistricting: Comparative and Theoretical Perspectives.* New York: Macmillan.

Cain, Bruce E., and Kenneth P. Miller. 2001. "The Populist Legacy: Initiatives and the Undermining of Representative Government." In *Dangerous Democracy? The Battle over Ballot Initiatives in America,* edited by Larry J. Sabato, Howard R. Ernst, and Bruce A. Larson. Lanham, Md.: Rowman and Littlefield.

Caltech MIT Voting Technology Project. 2001. *Voting: What Is What Could Be.* Pasadena, Calif.: California Institute of Technology; Cambridge: Massachusetts Institute of Technology.

Canon, David T. 1999. *Race, Redistricting and Representation.* Chicago: University of Chicago Press.

Caputo, Mara, and Ragan Naresh. 2001. "Despite Series of Court Rulings, State Officials Are Left Guessing." *Congressional Quarterly Weekly Report* 59 (August 11): 1970–71.

Ceaser, James W., and Andrew E. Busch. 2001. *The Perfect Tie: The True Story of the 2000 Presidential Election.* Lanham, Md.: Rowman and Littlefield.

*City of New York v. Department of Commerce.* 1994. 34 F.3d 114.

Coleman, John J. 1996. *Party Decline in America: Politics, Policy and the Fiscal State.* Princeton, N.J.: Princeton University Press.

Committee for the Study of the American Electorate. 2001. *Mobilization Propels Modest Turnout Increase.* Washington, D.C.: Author.

*Congressional Quarterly Guide to American Government.* 1979. Washington, D.C.: Congressional Quarterly Press.

*Congressional Quarterly Weekly Report.* 1997. "North Carolina's Map Heads to Justice, Judges for OK." 55: 810.

Converse, Phillip E. 1974. "Comment on Burnham's 'Theory and Voting Research.'" *American Political Science Review* 68: 1024–27.

*Cook v. Gralike.* 2001. 99–929.

Corrado, Anthony. 1997. "Party Soft Money." In *Campaign Finance Reform: A Sourcebook,* edited by Anthony Corrado, Thomas E. Mann, Daniel E. Ortiz, Trevor Potter, and Frank J. Sorauf. Washington, D.C.: Brookings Institution Press.

Cox, Gary W. 1987. *The Efficient Secret: The Cabinet and the Development of Political Parties in Victorian England.* Cambridge: Cambridge University Press.

Cronin, Thomas E. 1989. *Direct Democracy: The Politics of Initiative, Referendum and Recall.* Cambridge, Mass.: Harvard University Press.

Crotty, William. 2001. "Elections by Judicial Fiat: The Courts Decide." In *America's Choice 2000,* edited by William Crotty. Boulder, Colo.: Westview.

Dahl, Robert. 1994. *The New American Political (Dis)order.* Berkeley, Calif.: Institute of Governmental Studies Press.

Dash, Hal. [1997] 2001. Interview by Todd Donovan. Cited in "Political Consultants and the Initiative Industrial Complex," by Todd Donovan, Shaun Bowler, and David S. McCuan. In *Dangerous Democracy? The Battle over Ballot Initiatives in America,* edited by Larry J. Sabato, Howard R. Ernst, and Bruce A. Larson. Lanham, Md.: Rowman and Littlefield.

*Department of Commerce v. U.S. House of Representatives.* 1999. 142 L. Ed. 2d 797.

DeSipio, Louis. 2000. "United States." In *Introduction to Comparative Politics,* 2d edition, edited by Mark Kesselman, Joel Krieger, and William A. Joseph. Boston: Houghton Mifflin.

Diamond, Martin. 1977. *The Electoral College and the American Idea of Democracy.* Washington, D.C.: American Enterprise Institute.

Donovan, Todd, Shaun Bowler, and David S. McCuan. 2001. "Political Consultants and the Initiative Industrial Complex." In *Dangerous Democracy? The Battle over Ballot Initiatives in America,* edited by Larry J. Sabato, Howard R. Ernst, and Bruce A. Larson. Lanham, Md.: Rowman and Littlefield.

Donovan, Todd, Shaun Bowler, David McCuan, and Ken Fernandez. 1998. "Contending Players and Strategies: Opposition Advantages in Initiative Elections." In *Citizens as Legislators: Direct Democracy in the United States,* edited by Shaun Bowler, Todd Donovan, and Caroline J. Tolbert. Columbus: Ohio State University Press.

Doppelt, Jack, and Ellen Shearer. 1999. *Nonvoters: America's No Shows.* Beverly Hills, Calif.: Sage Publications.

Dudley, Robert L., and Alan R. Gitelson. 2002. *American Elections: The Rules Matter.* New York: Longman.

Dunleavy, Patrick, and Helen Margetts. 1995. "Understanding the Dynamics of Electoral Reform." *International Political Science Review* 16: 9–29.

Durbin, Thomas M. 2001. "The Electoral College Method of Electing the President and Vice President and Proposals for Reform." In *The Electoral College and Presidential Elections,* edited by Alexandra Kura. Huntington, N.Y.: Nova Science Publishers.

Ellis, Richard J. 2002. *Democratic Delusions: The Initiative Process in America.* Lawrence: University Press of Kansas.

Ernst, Howard R. 2001. "The Historical Role of Narrow-Material Interests in Initiative Politics." In *Dangerous Democracy? The Battle over Ballot Initiatives in America,* edited by Larry J. Sabato, Howard R. Ernst, and Bruce A. Larson. Lanham, Md.: Rowman and Littlefield.

Farrell, David M. 1997. *Comparing Electoral Systems.* Englewood Cliffs, N.J.: Prentice Hall.

———. 2001. *Electoral Systems: A Comparative Introduction.* New York: Palgrave.

Farris, Anne. 2001. *Electoral Reform: Moving from Crisis to Positive Change.* New York: Carnegie Corporation.

Fenno, Richard F. 1973. *Congressmen in Committees.* Boston: Little, Brown.

*First National Bank of Boston v. Bellotti.* 1978. 435 U.S. 765.

Fiorina, Morris P. 1999. "Extreme Voices: A Dark Side of Civic Engagement." In *Civic Engagement and American Democracy,* edited by Theda Skocpol and Morris P. Fiorina. Washington, D.C.: Brookings Institution Press.

Flanigan, William H., and Nancy H. Zingale. 1998. *Political Behavior of the American Electorate.* 9th edition. Washington, D.C.: Congressional Quarterly Press.

Forum on Election Reform. 2001. *Building Consensus on Election Reform.* Washington, D.C.: Constitution Project.

Franklin, Mark N. 1996. "Electoral Participation." In *Comparing Democracies: Elections and Voting in Global Perspective,* edited by Lawrence LeDuc, Richard G. Niemi, and Pippa Norris. Thousand Oaks, Calif.: Sage Publications.

Gallup Poll. 2000. Retrieved May 2, 2001, at http://pollinreport.com/wh2post.htm.

Gerber, Elizabeth R. 1999. *The Populist Paradox: Interest Group Influence and the Problem of Direct Democracy.* Princeton, N.J.: Princeton University Press.

Gerber, Elizabeth R., and Arthur Lupia. 1996. "Term Limits, Responsiveness, and the Failure of Increased Competition." In *Legislative Term Limits: Public Choice Perspectives,* edited by Bernard Grofman. New York: Kluwer Academic Publishers.

Ginsberg, Benjamin. 1982. *The Consequences of Consent: Elections, Citizen Control, and Popular Acquiescence.* New York: Random House.

Gonzalez, David. 2001. "African Americans Seek Inquiry into Florida Vote." In *36 Days: The Complete Chronicle of the 2000 Presidential Election Crisis.* New York: Times Books.

"Governor Signs Historic Election Reform into Law." 2001. Tallahassee: Office of the Governor of Florida.

Greenhouse, Linda. 1999. "A Fight on Redistricting Returns to the High Court." *New York Times,* 18 May, A21.

Guinier, Lani. 1991. "The Triumph of Tokenism—The Voting Rights Act and the Theory of Black Electoral Success." *Michigan Law Review* 89: 1077–1154.

Guth, James L. 2000. "Clinton, Impeachment and the Culture Wars." In *The Postmodern Presidency: Bill Clinton's Legacy in U.S. Politics,* edited by Steven E. Schier. Pittsburgh, Pa.: University of Pittsburgh Press.

Hamilton, Alexander. [1788] 1961. "Federalist #59." In *The Federalist Papers,* by Alexander Hamilton, James Madison, and John Jay, edited by Clinton Rossiter. New York: New American Library.

Hardaway, Robert M. 1994. *The Electoral College and the Constitution: The Case for Preserving Federalism.* Westport, Conn.: Praeger.

Harris, John F. 2000. "A Clouded Mirror: Bill Clinton, Polls and the Politics of Survival." In *The Postmodern Presidency: Bill Clinton's Legacy in U.S. Politics,* edited by Steven E. Schier. Pittsburgh, Pa.: University of Pittsburgh Press.

Haskell, John. 2001. *Direct Democracy or Representative Government? Dispelling the Populist Myth.* Boulder, Colo.: Westview.

Heclo, Hugh. 2000. "Campaigning and Governing: A Conspectus." In *The Permanent Campaign and Its Future,* edited by Norman Ornstein and Thomas Mann. Washington, D.C.: American Enterprise Institute.

Hermens, Ferdinand A. 1984. "Representation and Proportional Representation." In *Choosing an Electoral System: Issues and Alternatives,* edited by Arend Lijphart and Bernard Grofman. New York: Praeger.

Hibbing, John R., and Elizabeth Theiss-Morse. 1995. *Congress as Public Enemy: Public Attitudes Toward American Political Institutions.* Cambridge: Cambridge University Press.

Hicks, John D. 1931. *The Populist Revolt.* Minneapolis: University of Minnesota Press.

Hill, David B., and Norman Luttbeg. 1983. *Trends in American Electoral Behavior.* Itasca, Ill.: F. E. Peacock Publishers.

Hirczy, Wolfgang. 1995. "Exploring Near-Universal Turnout: The Case of Malta." *European Journal of Political Research* 27: 255–72.

Holmes, Steven A. 1997. "Tentative Pact Will Allow Census to Test the Sampling Method." *New York Times,* 1 November, A12.

House of Representatives. 1994. Committee on the Judiciary. Subcommittee on Civil and Constitutional Rights. *Voting Rights Roundtable.* 103d Congress, 2d. Session. May 11.

*Hunt v. Cromartie.* 1999. 119 Sup. Ct. 1545.

Jackman, Robert W., and Ross A. Miller. 1995. "Voter Turnout in Industrial Democracies since the 1980s." *Comparative Political Studies* 27 (4): 467–92.

Jacobson, Gary C. 1997. *The Politics of Congressional Elections.* 4th edition. New York: Longman.

Jenks, Jeremiah. 1896. "Political Party Machinery in the United States." *Chautauquan,* April–September.

Jones, Bill. 2001. "Initiative and Reform." In *The Battle over Citizen Lawmaking,* edited by M. Dane Waters. Durham, N.C.: Carolina Academic Press.

Katz, Richard L. 1996. "Party Organization and Finance." In *Comparing Democracies: Elections and Voting in Global Perspective,* edited by Lawrence LeDuc, Richard G. Niemi, and Pippa Norris. Thousand Oaks, Calif.: Sage Publications.

———. 1997. *Democracy and Elections.* New York: Oxford University Press.

Kelly, Michael. 2001. "McCain-Feingold's Fatal Flaws." *Washington Post,* 5 April, A27.

Key, V.O. 1961. *Public Opinion and American Democracy.* New York: Knopf.

King, Anthony. 1997. *Running Scared: Why America's Politicians Campaign Too Much and Govern Too Little.* New York: Free Press.

King, David C. 1997. "The Polarization of Political Parties and the Mistrust of Government." In *Why People Don't Trust Government,* edited by Joseph H. Nye, Phillip D. Zelikow, and David C. King. Cambridge, Mass.: Harvard University Press.

Kingdon, John W. 1989. *Congressmen's Voting Decisions.* 3d edition. Ann Arbor: University of Michigan Press.

Kleppner, Paul. 1982. *Who Voted? The Dynamics of Electoral Turnout 1879–1900.* New York: Praeger.

Kornbluth, Alan. 2000. *Why American Stopped Voting: The Decline of Participatory Democracy and the Emergence of Modern American Politics.* New York: New York University Press.

Kousser, Morgan. 1974. *The Shaping of Southern Politics: Suffrage Restriction and the Establishment of the One-Party South 1990–1910.* New Haven, Conn.: Yale University Press.

Ladd, Everett Carl. 1997. "The Status-Quo Election: Introduction." *Public Perspective* 8(1): 5.

Ladd, Everett Carl, with Karlyn Bowman. 1998. *What's Wrong: A Survey of American Satisfaction and Complaint.* Washington, D.C.: American Enterprise Institute.

La Raja, Ray. 2001. "Sources and Uses of Soft Money: What Do We Know?" In *A User's Guide to Campaign Finance Reform,* edited by Gerald C. Lubenow. Lanham, Md.: Rowman and Littlefield.

LeDuc, Lawrence, Robert Niemi, and Pippa Norris. 1996. *Comparing Democracies: Elections and Voting in Global Perspective.* Thousand Oaks, Calif.: Sage Publications.

Lijphart, Arend. 1997. "Unequal Participation: Democracy's Unresolved Dilemma." *American Political Science Review* 91: 1–24.

———. 1999. *Patterns of Democracy: Government Forms and Performance in Thirty-Six Countries.* New Haven, Conn.: Yale University Press.

Lipset, Seymour Martin, and Stein Rokkan. 1967. *Party Systems and Voting Alignments: Cross-National Perspectives.* New York: Free Press.

Locke, John. [1690]. 1993. "Second Treatise on Government." In *Political Writings of John Locke,* edited by David Wootton. New York: Penguin.

Longley, Lawrence D., and Neil Pierce. 1999. *The Electoral College Primer 2000.* New Haven, Conn.: Yale University Press.

Lublin, David Ian. 1997. *The Paradox of Representation: Racial Gerrymandering and Minority Interests in Congress.* Princeton, N.J.: Princeton University Press.

Lupia, Arthur. 1994. "Shortcuts versus Encyclopedias: Information and Voting Behavior in California Insurance Reform Elections." *American Political Science Review* 86: 390–403.

Lynch, Michael E., Sr. 1999. "The Mandate Myth: Why Presidential Elections are Not Public Policy Plebiscites." In *"We Get What We Vote For ... Or Do We?": The Impact of Elections on Governing,* edited by Paul E. Scheele. Westport, Conn.: Praeger.

Madison, James. [1787]. 1961. "Federalist #10." In *The Federalist Papers,* by Alexander Hamilton, James Madison, and John Jay, edited by Clinton Rossiter. New York: New American Library.

Magleby, David B. 1984. *Direct Legislation: Voting on Ballot Propositions in the United States.* Baltimore, Md.: Johns Hopkins University Press.

———. 2000. "Conclusions and Implications." In *Outside Money: Soft Money and Issue Advocacy in the 1998 Congressional Elections,* edited by David B. Magleby. Lanham, Md.: Rowman and Littlefield.

Mainwaring, Scott P. 1999. *Rethinking Party Systems in the Third Wave of Democratization: The Case of Brazil.* Palo Alto, Calif.: Stanford University Press.

Marcus, Ruth. 1998. "Off the Ballot, but in the Contest." *Washington Post,* 6 July, national weekly edition.

Mayer, William G. 2001. "Public Attitudes on Campaign Finance." In *A User's Guide to Campaign Finance Reform,* edited by Gerald C. Lubenow. Lanham, Md.: Rowman and Littlefield.

McCuan, David, Shaun Bowler, Todd Donovan, and Ken Fernandez. 1998. "California's Political Warriors: Campaign Professionals and the Initiative Process." In *Citizens as Legislators: Direct Democracy in the United States,* edited by Shaun Bowler, Todd Donovan, and Caroline J. Tolbert. Columbus: Ohio State University Press.

McDonald, Michael P., and Samuel L. Popkin. 2001. "The Myth of the 'Vanishing Voter.'" *American Political Science Review* 95: 963–74.

McGerr, Michael E. 1986. *The Decline of Popular Politics: The American North 1865–1928.* New York: Oxford University Press.

Milkis, Sidney M. 1993. *The President and the Parties: The Transformation of the American Party System since the New Deal.* New York: Oxford University Press.

Monmonier, Mark. 2001. *Bushmanders and Bullwinkles: How Politicians Manipulate Electronic Maps and Census Data to Win Elections.* Chicago: University of Chicago Press.

Nather, David. 2002. "Election Overhaul May Have to Wait in Line Behind Other 'Crisis' Issues." *Congressional Quarterly Weekly Report* 60 (July 27): 2034–35.

National Association for the Advancement of Colored People. 1994. "Report of the NAACP Legal Defense and Education Fund: The Effect of Section 2 of the Voting Rights Act on the 1994 Congressional Elections." Mimeograph.

National Commission on Federal Election Reform. 2001. *To Assure Pride and Confidence in the Electoral Process.* Washington, D.C.: Brookings Institution Press.

*National Election Study.* 1996. Ann Arbor, Mich.: Institute for Social Research, Center for Political Studies.

———. 2000. Ann Arbor, Mich.: Institute for Social Research, Center for Political Studies.

National Task Force on Election Reform. 2001. *Election 2000: Review and Recommendations by the Nation's Elections Administrators.* Houston, Tex.: Election Center.

Nelson, Michael. 2001. "The Postelection Election: Politics by Other Means." In *The Elections of 2000,* edited by Michael Nelson. Washington, D.C.: Congressional Quarterly Press.

Neuman, W. Russell. 1986. *The Paradox of Mass Politics: Knowledge and Opinion in the American Electorate.* Cambridge, Mass.: Harvard University Press.

*Newsweek* Poll. 2001, December 14–15. Retrieved March 2, 2002, at http://pollingreport.com/wh2post.htm.

Nie, Norman H., Sidney Verba, and John R. Petrocik. 1976. *The Changing American Voter.* Cambridge, Mass.: Harvard University Press.

Nye, Joseph H., Phillip D. Zelikow, and David C. King. 1997. *Why People Don't Trust Government.* Cambridge, Mass.: Harvard University Press.

Ornstein, Norman J. 2001. "Eight Modest Ideas for Meaningful Campaign Finance Reform." In *A User's Guide to Campaign Finance Reform,* edited by Gerald C. Lubenow. Lanham, Md.: Rowman and Littlefield.

Ostrogorski, Moisei. 1902. *Democracy and the Organization of Political Parties.* 2 vols. Translated by Frederick Clark. New York: Macmillan.

Perez-Pena, Richard. 2001. "Bush Files Suit to Restore Rejected Military Ballots." In *36 Days: The Complete Chronicle of the 2000 Presidential Election Crisis.* New York: Times Books.

Petrocik, John R., and Scott W. Desposato. 1998. "The Partisan Consequences of Majority-Minority Redistricting in the South 1992 and 1994." *Journal of Politics* 60: 613–33.

Pierce, Neil R., and Lawrence D. Longley. 1981. *The People's President: The Electoral College in American History and the Direct Vote Alternative.* New Haven, Conn.: Yale University Press.

Political Staff of the *Washington Post.* 2001. *Deadlock: The Inside Story of America's Closest Election.* New York: PublicAffairs.

Pomper, Gerald M. 1997, October 8. "Campaign Finance." Message posted to H-Net forum on Antipartyism and Campaign Finance. Available at http://h-net.msu.edu.

Pomper, Gerald M., and Susan S. Lederman. 1980. *Elections in America.* 2d edition. New York: Longman.

"Pondering the Fate and Consequence of the Electoral College." 2000. *FoxNews.com.* Retrieved December 4, 2000, at http://foxnews.com/election_night/120300/electoral_college.smi.

Potter, Trevor. 1997. "Issue Advocacy and Express Advocacy." In *Campaign Finance Reform: A Sourcebook,* edited by Anthony Corrado, Thomas E. Mann, Daniel R. Ortiz, Trevor Potter, and Frank J. Sorauf. Washington, D.C.: Brookings Institution Press.

Powell, G. Bingham. 1986. "American Voter Turnout in Comparative Perspective." *American Political Science Review* 89: 19–43.

———. 2000. *Elections as Instruments of Democracy: Majoritarian and Proportional Visions.* New Haven, Conn.: Yale University Press.

Prewitt, Kenneth. 2000. "Political Science for Design of a Sensible Census." [Electronic version] *PS: Political Science and Politics* (June). Retrieved March 3, 2001, at http://apsanet.org/PS/june00/prewitt.cfm.

Pruden, Wesley. 2001. "Getting Punch Drunk on Disappointment." *Washington Times,* 9 March, A4.

Przeworski, Adam, Susan C. Stokes, and Bernard Manin, eds. 1999. *Democracy, Accountability and Representation.* Cambridge: Cambridge University Press.

Rauch, Jonathan. 1994. *Demosclerosis: The Silent Killer of American Government.* New York: Times Books.

Raskin, Jamin B. 2001. "A Right to Vote." *American Prospect,* August 27, 10–12.

*Reynolds v. Sims.* 1964. 377 U.S. 533.

Riker, William H. 1982. *Liberalism against Populism: A Confrontation between the Theory of Democracy and the Theory of Social Choice.* Prospect Heights, Ill.: Waveland Press.

———. 1986. *The Art of Political Manipulation.* New Haven, Conn.: Yale University Press.

Riordan, William. 1963. *Plunkitt of Tammany Hall.* New York: E. P. Dutton.

Ritchie, Rob, Steven Hill, and Caleb Kleppner. 2000. "Reclaiming Democracy in the 21st Century: Instant Runoffs, Proportional Representation and Cumulative Voting." *Social Policy* (winter): 35–42.

Roche, John P. 1961. "The Founding Fathers: A Reform Caucus in Action." *American Political Science Review* 55: 796–810.

Rosen, Jeffrey. 2000. "Talk Is Cheap." *New Republic,* 14 February, 20–22.

Rosenstone, Steven J., and John Mark Hansen. 1993. *Mobilization, Participation and Democracy in America.* New York: Macmillan.

Rosenthal, Alan. 1998. *The Decline of Representative Democracy: Process, Participation and Power in State Legislatures.* Washington, D.C.: Congressional Quarterly Press.

Rusk, Jerrold. 1970. "Effect of the Australian Ballot Reform on Split-Ticket Voting: 1876–1908." *American Political Science Review* 64: 1220–38.

———. 1974. "Comment: The American Electoral Universe: Speculation and Evidence." *American Political Science Review* 68: 1028–49.

Sabato, Larry J. 1984. *The Rise of the Political Consultants: New Ways of Winning Elections.* New York: Basic Books.

———. 1989. *Paying for Elections: The Campaign Finance Thicket.* New York: Twentieth Century Fund.

Sayre, Wallace S., and Judith H. Parris. 1970. *Voting for President.* Washington, D.C.: Brookings Institution Press.

Schattschneider, Elmer Eric. 1977. *Party Government.* Westport, Conn.: Greenwood.

Schier, Steven E. 2000. *By Invitation Only: The Rise of Exclusive Politics in the United States.* Pittsburgh: University of Pittsburgh Press.

Schrag, Peter. 1998. *Paradise Lost: California's Experience, America's Future.* New York: New Press.

———. 2001. "The Extension of Politics by Other Means." In *The Battle over Citizen Lawmaking,* edited by M. Dane Waters. Durham, N.C.: Carolina Academic Press.

Schudson, Michael. 1978. *Discovering the News: A Social History of American Newspapers.* New York: Basic Books.

———. 1998. *The Good Citizen: A History of American Civic Life.* New York: Free Press.

Schultz, Jim. 1996. *The Initiative Cookbook: Recipes and Stories from California's Ballot Wars.* San Francisco: Democracy Center.

Schumpeter, Joseph A. 1976. *Capitalism, Socialism and Democracy.* New York: Harper and Row.

Seelye, Katharine Q. 2001. "California Is Phasing Out Punch Card Voting." *New York Times,* 20 September, A16.

Sellers, Patrick J., David T. Canon, and Matthew M. Schousen. 1998. "Congressional Redistricting in North Carolina." In *Race and Redistricting in the 1990s,* edited by Bernard Grofman. New York: Agathon Press.

Semetko, Holli A. 1996. "The Media." In *Comparing Democracies: Elections and Voting in Global Perspective,* edited by Lawrence LeDuc, Richard G. Niemi, and Pippa Norris. Thousand Oaks, Calif.: Sage Publications.

*Shaw v. Hunt.* 1996. 116 Sup. Ct. 1894.

*Shaw v. Reno.* 1993. 61 L.W. 4818.

Silbey, Joel H. 1991. *The American Political Nation, 1838–1893.* Stanford, Calif.: Stanford University Press.

Sniderman, Paul, Richard A. Brody, and Phillip E. Tetlock. 1991. *Reasoning and Choice: Explorations in Political Psychology.* New York: Cambridge University Press.

"Some Winners Obvious, Others Less So." 2002, March 20. [Electronic version] *USA Today.* Retrieved March 21, 2002, at http://usatoday.com/news/washdc/2002/03/20/finance-winners-losers.

Sorauf, Frank J. 1992. *Inside Campaign Finance: Myths and Realities.* New Haven, Conn.: Yale University Press.

Starr, Paul. 1998. "The Loophole We Can't Close." *American Prospect* 36: 22–26.

State Senate of Florida. 2001. *Senate Bill 1118.* May 5.

Stevens, John Paul. 2001. "Dissenting Opinion." In *Bush v. Gore: The Court Cases and the Commentary,* edited by E. J. Dionne and William Kristol. Washington, D.C.: Brookings Institution Press.

Sunstein, Cass. 2001. *Republic.com*. Princeton, N.J.: Princeton University Press.

Swain, Carol M. 1993. "The Future of Black Representation." *American Prospect* 19: 78–83.

Texeira, Ruy. 1992. *The Disappearing American Voter*. Washington, D.C.: Brookings Institution Press.

*Thornburg v. Gingles*. 1986. 478 U.S. 30.

Troy, Gil. 1991. *See How They Ran: The Changing Role of the Presidential Candidate*. New York: Free Press.

Van Natta, Don, Jr., and Dana Canedy. 2001. "The Case of the Butterfly Ballot." In *36 Days: The Complete Chronicle of the 2000 Presidential Election Crisis*. New York: Times Books.

Verba, Sidney. 1996. "The Citizen as Respondent: Sample Surveys and American Democracy." *American Political Science Review* 90: 1–7.

Verba, Sidney, Kay Lehman Schlozman, and Henry E. Brady. 1997. *Voice and Equality: Civic Voluntarism in American Politics*. Cambridge, Mass.: Harvard University Press.

Verba, Sidney, Norman H. Nie, and Jae On Kim. 1978. *Participation and Political Equality: A Four-Nation Comparison*. Chicago: University of Chicago Press.

Wand, Jonathan N., Kenneth W. Shotts, Jasjeet S. Sekhon, Walter R. Mebane, Jr., Michael C. Herron, and Henry E. Brady. 2001. "The Butterfly Did It: The Aberrant Vote for Buchanan in Palm Beach County, Florida." *American Political Science Review* 95: 793–810.

Ware, Alan. 1988. *The Breakdown of Democratic Party Organization, 1940–1980*. New York: Oxford University Press.

Wawro, Gregory. 2001. "A Panel Probit Analysis of Campaign Contributions and Roll Call Votes." *American Journal of Political Science* 41: 563–579.

*Wesberry v. Sanders*. 1964. 376 U.S. 1.

Whitaker, L. Paige. 2001. *The Electoral College: An Overview and Analysis of Reform Proposals*. Washington, D.C.: Congressional Research Service.

Wilson, Graham K. 1998. *Only in America? The Politics of the United States in Comparative Perspective*. New York: Chatham House.

*Wisconsin v. City of New York*. 1996. 517 U.S. 1.

Wolfinger, Raymond, and Steven J. Rosenstone. 1980. *Who Votes?* New Haven, Conn.: Yale University Press.

Zaller, John. 1992. *The Nature and Origins of Mass Opinion*. Cambridge: Cambridge University Press.

Zimmerman, Bill. [1997] 2001. Interview by Todd Donovan. Cited in "Political Consultants and the Initiative Industrial Complex," by Todd Donovan, Shaun Bowler, and David S. McCuan. In *Dangerous Democracy? The Battle over Ballot Initiatives in America*, edited by Larry J. Sabato, Howard R. Ernst, and Bruce A. Larson. Lanham, Md.: Rowman and Littlefield.

# Index

accountability, 24–25; apportionment/
redistricting and, 126; campaign spending and, 51; electoral administration
and, 112–13, 125–26; electoral college
and, 103–7, 125; factors enhancing,
31–32; impact of electoral systems
compared, 51–53; initiatives and, 79;
legislative politics vs. initiatives, 95;
mixed electoral systems and, 48; as
objective of an electoral system, 28;
party government and, 34–35; Progressive reforms and, 66; proportional
representation systems and, 43–44;
recalls and, 80; referendums and, 80;
single-member majority systems and,
41–42; single-member plurality systems
and, 37, 39; single-transferable-vote
systems and, 46; voter turnout and,
74–75
activists and activation: impact of, 16–17;
targeted in initiatives, 90; vs. mobilization of voters, 68–71. *See also* initiatives;
issue advocacy
Adams, John Quincy, 99
AFL-CIO, 97
African Americans, racial redistricting and.
*See* redistricting
agenda control, 21, 79–80, 90
Aldrich, John, 59
Allswang, John, 84–85
American public: apathy of, 19, 29; attitudes of nonvoters, 70–71; dislike of

political debate, 15–17, 28; election of
2000, acceptance of, 8, 98, 101; electoral
salience and, 72; initiative process,
support for, 78–79; legislative process,
opinion of, 93–94; national institutions,
reverence for, 19–20; political knowledge of (*see* knowledge)
Americans for Medical Rights, 89
Anderson, John, 103
Ansolabehere, Stephen, 132, 135
apathy, 19, 29
apportionment, 115, 138. *See also* decennial
census
Australia, 40–42, 44–45, 53, 71
Austria, 71

Bachrach, Peter, 29
*Baker v. Carr,* 119
ballots: in Florida, 4, 6; proposals for
improving, 138; questions regarding, 112;
types of, 110–11; uniquely American, 34
Barber, Benjamin, 29, 142–44
Belgium, 71
Berelson, Bernard, 73–74
Bessette, Joseph, 15
Bowler, Shaun, 82
Breyer, Stephen G., 122
Britain. *See* Great Britain
Bryan, William Jennings, 66
Buchanan, Pat, 3, 147
*Buckley v. Valeo,* 49–50, 129, 131, 134–35
Burke, Edmund, 52